MERCURY AND ME

MERCURY AND *Me*

Jim Hutton
WITH TIM WAPSHOTT

BLOOMSBURY

LONDON · NEW DELHI · NEW YORK · SYDNEY

First published in Great Britain 1994

This paperback edition published 1995

Bloomsbury Publishing plc, 50 Bedford Square, London WC1B 3DP

www.bloomsbury.com

Bloomsbury Publishing, London, New Delhi, New York and Sydney

PICTURE SOURCES
Richard Young *page* 5 bottom, 6 *top*, 11 *top*
All other pictures courtesy of Jim Hutton

A CIP catalogue record for this book is available from the British Library

ISBN 978 0 7475 2134 1

10 9 8 7 6

Typeset by Hewer Text UK Ltd, Edinburgh
Printed and bound in Great Britain by CPI Group (UK) Ltd, Croydon CR0 4YY

CONTENTS

For my family,
Martha and Stephen

ACKNOWLEDGEMENTS

There are many people I would like to thank for helping me get this project off the ground. First and foremost, I would like to thank Dominic Denny for all his endeavours on my behalf. Without him there would be no book.

Next, I should like to thank Tim Wapshott for helping me channel my thoughts. I should also like to thank my literary agent Giles Gordon at Sheil Land Associates.

There are so many I feel I would like to acknowledge for supporting me and my book but, before doing so, first may I apologise to anyone I omit by accident. So, my heartfelt thanks to the following: John Alexander, Dr Gordon Atkinson, Liz Bennett, Bloomsbury Publishing plc, John Deacon, Joe Fennelli, Leslie Freestone, Peter Freestone, Terry Giddings, Julian Hedley, Robert Kirby, Sonia Land, Debbie Leng, Philip Loveday, Brian May, Billy Mullen, John Rowell, Dominique Taylor, Roger Taylor, Nicholas Wapshott, Misa Watanabe and, last but by no means least, Jackie Gunn and all the members of the Queen Fan Club.

Finally, most of the photographs which appear in this book are from my own collection. However, I would like to thank Richard Young and Misa Watanabe for additional pictures.

Jim Hutton
London W12
August 1994

FOREWORD

Freddie Mercury was unique. Before I continue I admit that I am biased. During my twelve years as his personal assistant I learned more from him about art, furniture, porcelain and many more things than I could have ever been taught in any amount of lectures. Freddie's enthusiasm for life was infectious.

I consider myself lucky to have been there with him during the good times and, although I would have preferred a different ending, I also consider myself lucky that I was one of the few he wanted with him in the final days. He was a musical genius, strong-willed, obstinate, soft-centred, caring and, above all, genuine.

One of the others was Jim Hutton, whom I have known for over twenty years. We first met across a busy restaurant counter in Selfridge's, the department store, in 1973. Then we lost contact until I turned up at Freddie's flat one evening for dinner and there was Jim. We hadn't seen each other for a few years, but it seemed no more than a few weeks.

Freddie and Jim were certainly an odd couple. Because of their temperaments, life around Freddie and Jim was never what you could call easy. But at least it was never boring.

What follows will, I am sure, be of great interest. It gives a previously unseen insight into someone about whom so much has been written. It has never been in Jim's nature to be anything other than straightforward.

Peter Freestone
London SW1
August 1994

1

FREDDIE WHO?

It had been just another ordinary weekend in London towards the end of 1983. I'd spent much of it drinking in gay pubs and clubs with my lover, John Alexander. He was a stocky lad with dark hair and I was besotted with him. Sunday night we ended up in a gay club called Cocobana, in the basement of a hotel in South Kensington, west London, and it was my first time in the place.

We were standing near the bar, drinking lager from cans. The club was fairly busy and plenty of anonymous faces were milling around or dancing to the disco beats thundering out from the speakers.

I suppose I was on my fourth lager when it happened. John went to the lavatory and this guy came up to me. I was thirty-four and he was slightly older. He was dressed casually in jeans and a white vest and, like me, had a moustache. He was slight and not the sort of man I found attractive. I preferred men bigger and butcher.

'Let me buy you a drink,' he said.

I had an almost full can and I replied: 'No, thank you.' Then he asked me what I was doing that night.

'Fuck off,' I said. 'You'd better ask my boyfriend about that.' The stranger could see he was getting nowhere with me and let the matter drop, going back to join his friends in the corner.

'Somebody's just tried to chat me up,' I told John when he returned.

'Who was he?' he asked. 'Which one?'

'Over there,' I said, pointing him out.

'That's Freddie Mercury!' he said, although it meant nothing to me – not a light. If he'd been the managing director of the Savoy Hotel where I worked it might have been a different matter. But I never kept up with popular music. Although I had it on the radio all the time, I couldn't tell one group from another, or one singer from another. I had never heard of Queen. John wasn't annoyed that Freddie had tried it on – on the contrary, he was flattered that a famous singer fancied his partner.

John and I carried on drinking until the place closed around midnight, then we headed home to our house in Clapham, south London. Early next morning I was back at work, as a gentlemen's hairdresser at the Savoy Hotel's small barber's shop concession.

Four or five months after that night in the gay club Cocobana John took me out to dinner at a swanky restaurant, September's in Fulham, west London.

I was sitting with my back to the door and we ate a delicious meal. I was happy with life, quite content with my lot. Then John, looking over my shoulder, said: 'Oh, your friend is here.'

'Who?' I asked.

'Freddie Mercury,' he said. 'The guy who tried to chat you up a few months ago at Cocobana.'

I looked around, trying not to be noticed doing so, and indeed there was the same man dining with friends. I don't think he saw me.

Not long after, John and I moved to Sutton in Surrey where we rented rooms. Our landlady, Mrs Ivy Taverner, was in her seventies and John and I shared the two attic rooms at the top of her semi-detached house. It was a modest place: a bedroom, sitting room and basic cooking facilities on the landing.

But after a while we found we needed more space and we began getting on one another's nerves. I didn't expect much out of life but I was desperate for an harmonious, loving relationship. I became too possessive of John and he eventually saw me as a ball and chain; he was yearning for his freedom. In the spring of 1984, after two years together, we split up. I kept the rooms, and John moved out; we've remained friends.

I worked at the barber's shop five days a week and every other Saturday morning. In the week I left work around six and by the time I'd got home – forty-five minutes by train from Victoria Station – and cooked myself something to eat most of the evening had gone.

I led a quiet life on my own at Ivy Taverner's. Once in a while I might meet a friend in Sutton for a drink, but usually I kept very much to myself. I'm not a promiscuous person and never went out deliberately to pick someone up. I liked my own company more than other people's. Occasionally I'd meet somebody and we might have a fling, but my philosophy was always 'If it happens, it happens; if it doesn't, it doesn't.' I got into the habit of going out once a week, on Thursdays as that was pay-day, to the Market Tavern, a gay pub in Vauxhall, south London. It was a long way to go from Sutton for a drink, but I regarded it as my 'local'. I always stood in the same little corner at the bar, eying-up the bar staff with my pint before me and my packet of cigarettes neatly rolled into my sleeve. I'd stand there all night on the exact same spot, drinking a few pints and taking in the atmosphere, oblivious to everyone else. I was kept entertained by watching a bunch of strangers enjoying themselves.

When the summer months came along, it became too dull for whole weekends in Sutton so I switched my drinking night to Saturdays. I always thought I was out totally alone on those nights. Not so, apparently. Many years later, after Freddie's death, I had a heart-to-heart with Joe Fannelli, a former lover of Freddie's and his live-in chef, confessor and confidant. Although Freddie had a flat in London, throughout 1984 he was mostly living in Munich, Germany. Whenever he was back in London for a weekend he'd invariably end up in Heaven, the gay nightclub under Charing Cross Station.

I don't know how, but Freddie discovered where I drank. On his way to Heaven he would tell his chauffeur, a guy called Gary, to take a detour via the Market Tavern. Freddie's old Mercedes would draw up and Joe was instructed to see if I was on my mark at the bar. Once he'd reported back to Freddie that, indeed, this creature of habit was in place, they'd continue their journey to Heaven for the night.

If you're Irish, which I am, then 17 March is a date which never leaves your mind: St Patrick's Day. In 1985, 17 March fell on a Sunday, and the night before I'd been drinking in the Market Tavern with a few Irish friends. We all agreed to meet up again at the pub the next day at lunchtime. I rarely drink at lunchtime, but that day I made an exception; the afternoon soon became the evening and eventually I left for Sutton and bed. I had to go to work the next morning. I'd have probably cut someone's throat when shaving them if I'd stayed drinking any longer.

That particular Paddy's Day is ingrained in my memory, so I know it was the following Saturday, 23 March, that I met Freddie again. The day started much like any other. I made myself some supper, then headed out dressed appropriately for the gay scene – jeans and white vest. The look at the time was 'High Clone', complete with mandatory moustache. I got the tube to Vauxhall and, climbing three steps at a time, put my knees and arse out of my jeans. They completely ripped.

When the Market Tavern closed, I fell straight into the back of a minicab, driven by a regular face who was used to me slurring Sutton as my destination. That night I decided I wanted to go on partying and told him to drive me to Heaven instead. It was a very occasional haunt of mine; I'd always found it too big and impersonal for my liking.

I arrived fairly late, legless and undoubtedly on another planet. Worse still, after paying the minicab I only had £5 to my name. At least I didn't have to pay to get in, as I discovered that a friend was on the door. I went straight to the downstairs bar and ordered a pint of lager.

'Let me buy you this,' said a voice. I looked up. It was the chap from the Cocobana in 1983. Freddie Thing. I'd had a fair amount to drink. My tongue had loosened up. My defences were down.

'No, I'll buy you one,' I said.

'A large vodka tonic,' came the reply. There went my fiver in one go. If I was lucky I would be left with a little over £1, perhaps enough to get the night bus back to Sutton.

'How big's your dick?' Freddie asked, laughing. It was, I later learned, a typically outrageous Freddie opening gambit.

I don't like answering such personal questions, so I said: 'It's none of your business!' If I hadn't been so drunk I'd have told him to fuck off. But I did reprimand him on his accent, a sort of mid-Atlantic drawl.

'For God's sake, drop the phoney American accent,' I said.

'I haven't got an American accent,' he answered. He introduced himself as 'Freddie'. I knew he was Freddie Mercury, but still had little inkling who he actually was, nor what he did. It didn't seem to matter.

Freddie asked me to join his crowd of friends, who were grouped in the middle of the bar. Joe Fannelli was there, and Peter Straker, the singer, with a couple of others. Joe was fair-haired, worked out and was in his thirties, with a cautious approach to people and life. I haven't got a clue what any of us talked about that night; I let them do most of the talking.

A little later Freddie whispered in my ear: 'Come on, let's go and dance.' We made straight for the dance floor. I was a bit of a raver in those days, if sufficiently well oiled. I'd get up and dance even by myself if the mood took me – tearing the floor to bits along with anyone unlucky enough to be in my way. For a few good hours I threw Freddie across the floor. I think he admired my unselfconscious, bullish dancing.

By about four in the morning Freddie decided he'd had

enough and we were all invited back to his flat at 12 Stafford Terrace, Kensington. I sat next to him in the back of the car.

Freddie's home was the lower part of a house conversion. The hallway and dining room were on ground level and the kitchen on the mezzanine. In the basement were the bedrooms – Freddie's facing the street and Joe Fannelli's at the rear – and a large sitting room looking out on to a small, patioed garden.

Outside, the dawn was almost up, but everyone in that flat was in the mood to keep partying. At one point Freddie offered me some cocaine, but it wasn't my scene. 'No, thanks,' I said. 'I don't touch the stuff.' I'd had the odd joint of cannabis in my time, but never anything harder.

Anyway, I was already happily tanked up and more interested in playing with Freddie's two cats, Tiffany and Oscar, than putting anything up my nose. Despite a room full of noisy people, Freddie and I flirted all the time. There was a lot of eye contact with the odd wink, or nod, or touch.

Eventually Freddie and I fell into his bed, too drunk to do anything more than fumble about with each other to little effect. Freddie cuddled up to me affectionately. We both nattered away until we finally flaked out. Next morning we lay entwined, carrying on talking where we'd left off. When we got around to discussing what each of us did for a living, I told him I was a hairdresser. He said, 'I'm a singer.' Then he offered to go and make me a cup of tea.

Later, around noon as I was leaving the flat, Freddie gave me his telephone number. 'Fair dues,' I said. 'Here's mine.' I didn't hear a word from Freddie after that night, and thought no more of it.

Then three months later, in the early summer, he did get in touch. I got home on a Friday and started cooking bangers, mash, marrowfat peas and fried onions. I'd just put the potatoes on to boil when the phone went downstairs in the hall. Mrs Taverner answered it and called up for me.

I trundled down and the voice at the other end simply said: 'Guess who this is?'

I tried a few names without success.

'It's Freddie,' he said. 'I'm having a little dinner party. Come over.'

'I can't,' I replied. 'I've just started cooking my dinner.'

'Well, turn everything off at once,' he demanded insistently. 'Come over. You'll have a good time, I promise.'

So I turned off my bangers and set off for Freddie's flat. I had no bottle of wine to offer my host but felt I should take something along, as a present, so when I got to Victoria Station I bought Freddie two £1.99 bunches of freesias.

Then I caught a bus to Kensington High Street and walked towards his flat. 'This is silly. I'm going nuts!' I thought to myself. I'd never taken flowers to a guy before and had really surprised myself when I bought them. Besides, they looked half dead. As I turned into Stafford Terrace I spotted a bin and, embarrassed by the flowers, threw them in. Little did I know that freesias were one of Freddie's favourite flowers. If I'd actually given them to him that day, he'd have gone crazy.

So when Freddie opened the front door to me, I just gave him a big smile. We hugged and went downstairs to the sitting room to meet his other guests. There were about six of them.

I felt apprehensive about meeting Freddie's friends. As we were going upstairs to the dining room, one of the guests put his hand on my shoulder and acted hurt.

'All right,' he said. 'Ignore me.'

'Jesus!' I said. I had to look twice. It was Peter Freestone, a former colleague from my pre-Savoy days at Selfridge's, the Oxford Street department store. In those days I was working as a hairpiece sales assistant while Peter managed the ground floor Orchard Room restaurant. Later he worked at the Royal Opera House as a dresser. Now he helped Freddie manage his life and was constantly on call.

Peter was in his early thirties. Well over six feet tall, he towered over everyone, large and stocky. He had a chubby face and a warm smile. I could tell there wasn't a bad bone in his body.

Freddie and the others always called Peter 'Phoebe'. Freddie loved finding nicknames – usually gender-swapping ones – for those around him. His own was Melina, after Melina Mercouri, the volatile Greek actress and Joe was Liza, as in 'Liza Fannelli'. (Although I've called my book *Mercury and Me*, I only ever called him Freddie all the time we were together.)

At supper I sat next to Freddie. He had hit the cocaine again at some point, and couldn't stop talking. He was buzzing so much he could have talked to the wall.

After supper we headed out to Heaven for a few hours, then, exhausted, we went back to Stafford Terrace. All Freddie's other guests, especially a guy called Paul Prenter, were trying to find out what they could about me.

I didn't feel at all at ease with Prenter. He was a slight man with a moustache and glasses. His eyes constantly darted around the room, watching everyone around him and everything going on. He didn't miss a trick. He was very talkative but also had a bitchy streak in him.

There was a lot of bitchiness among Freddie's friends. They seemed to compete constantly for his attention. None of them had ever seen me out on the gay scene. Unlike most of Freddie's previous boyfriends, I was a total stranger. And I remained a tight-lipped mystery to them. They knew my name, where I lived and what I did for a living, but no more. When they asked questions, I was as evasive as possible. It was none of their damned business!

Freddie didn't ask any questions. We picked up exactly where we'd left off three months earlier. I hadn't heard from him in that time, and that night he explained why it had been so long. After our previous liaison he'd gone back to his flat in Munich. It was his real home, because at the time he was living out of Britain as a tax exile. He'd also been on a tour of Australia, New Zealand and Japan with his group, Queen.

In January Queen had headlined the world's biggest rock festival, Rock in Rio, in Rio de Janeiro, Brazil. By all accounts the trip had been a riot for Freddie. He told me he had travelled everywhere in an armoured car with police outriders, sometimes speeding the wrong way down one-way streets. One policeman kept trying to make him laugh – by shoving his loaded gun down his trousers. And when Freddie slipped from the hotel with Joe to go shopping they were mobbed by fans and locked in a shop for their own safety until security men could spirit them away. Even the great South American footballer Diego Maradona turned out to be a Queen fan, and when he met Freddie he gave him his football shirt.

At the Rio concert Freddie almost made a terrible mistake when he made his entrance to sing 'I Want to Break Free' in drag with huge plastic breasts. Brazilians had adopted the song as their liberation anthem and took offence at what he was wearing. Things began to turn nasty until he quickly whipped the outfit off.

One tune I recognised was Freddie's solo debut single, 'Love Kills'. It had been a huge hit in the gay clubs in London at the end of 1984. He had just released his first solo album *Mr Bad Guy*, dedicated to his cats, and his second single 'I Was Born to Love You'.

While Freddie told me the story of his life that summer we discovered there was a special chemistry between us. I fell in love with so much about Freddie, regardless of what he did for a living. He had big brown eyes and a vulnerable, child-like persona. He was quite the opposite of the sort of man I'd ever fancied before: I liked big men with stocky legs, but Freddie had a waspish figure and the thinnest legs I'd ever seen. And for all that he had apparently achieved, he appeared to be remarkably insecure. He seemed totally sincere, and I was hooked.

Freddie said he had taken a shine to me when he'd first seen me because I reminded him of a favourite pin-up: Burt

Reynolds! He liked his men big and strong, as long as they were softies at heart.

After three months' silence, we were ready to begin our affair. I think I must have seemed something of a challenge to him: he was one of the biggest rock stars in the world and I didn't seem impressed by any of that side of his life.

We spent that night together. I left in the afternoon, before Freddie was driven to Heathrow to take a flight back to his home in Munich. My life went on in London, unchanged. I strolled down to Kensington High Street to wait for a bus to Victoria. I walked with my head bowed towards the ground as usual. But it wasn't because I was sad or miserable. Quite the contrary.

Freddie's car zoomed by, but I didn't notice. He told me later that he had spotted me and thought I looked downcast and it had made him upset. He'd said to Joe and his driver: 'There goes my man. Doesn't he look miserable?'

I wasn't miserable, I was just being me. All the same, Freddie said he'd been tempted to turn back and cheer me up.

The next day I was back at work at the Savoy and my life carried on as before, totally without incident. Then, on the Friday I got a call in the barber's shop from someone in the 'Queen Office', saying Freddie was expecting me to go to Germany that night to be with him. His chauffeur was being sent to pick me up from the Savoy after work to drive me to Heathrow. I panicked. I was completely broke.

'Sorry,' I said apologising to the stranger at the other end. 'I can't afford it. I can't afford fares like this.'

'You don't have to worry about that,' came the response. 'Your ticket has already been paid for.'

That night, after I had locked up the barber's shop at the Savoy, Freddie's chauffeur handed me a Lufthansa air ticket and I was soon flying off to Munich.

The flight was pretty special. It was the first time I'd ever travelled first-class and I had the compartment to myself, with four young attendants waiting on my every whim.

My feelings about the weekend were rather mixed. Although I was thrilled that he'd bought me a ticket I was a bit annoyed with him because I always like to pay my own way and remain under no obligation to anyone. For the first time I couldn't afford to be independent. I was a hairdresser on £70 a week.

When the plane touched down at Munich Airport, Freddie was waiting. He was with Joe and Barbara Valentin, a German actress who in her day had been Germany's answer to Brigitte Bardot and was now a cult heroine because of her work with the fashionable German film director Rainer Werner Fassbinder.

Freddie grabbed and hugged me. Such open affection embarrassed me dreadfully. That day the British tabloid press missed a fabulous photograph to throw over their front pages, but Freddie didn't care who saw him throw his arms around me. He felt that in Germany people were more tolerant and certainly no one at the airport batted an eyelid.

From the airport we drove the half-hour journey through the darkness to Freddie's apartment. As soon as we arrived he jumped on top of me. He hardly gave me time to put down my overnight bag before we made love and we continued for half an hour or so. I would learn that he was very impulsive about sex which, fortunately, we both enjoyed thoroughly. When he got the urge for sex there was no stopping it – he wanted it at once. He was a very sexy man and I think I partly fell in love, much to my own surprise, with his amazingly slender body. His waist was just twenty-eight inches. The sex we had was raunchy but very gentle – nothing too acrobatic. Freddie could be either active or passive, but tended to be the latter throughout our relationship; it depended on the time of month! I think Freddie thought of it as making love in those early days, but I don't think it would be called lovemaking until some time later. For the time being it was just steamy sex.

When we re-emerged from the bedroom, Freddie showed me the rest of his flat. It had two bedrooms and was on the third floor of a four-storey block. It was bright and spacious, and sparsely but tastefully furnished. The dinner table sparkled, laid ready for supper. Before long Freddie's guests arrived, mainly English-speaking German friends. After supper we left for the gay bars in Munich's bohemian 'Bermuda Triangle' district. And finally we ended up in a wonderful club, New York New York.

Freddie was the club's regular star and one corner was exclusively reserved for him and his inner circle, who were reverently referred to as 'The Family'. Freddie had been at the cocaine again and by New York New York he had caught his second wind. As soon as I had had a few drinks and became a bit merry, I grabbed him and recklessly headed off to the dance floor.

That night Freddie made a great fuss of me and showed me off to his friends. I was surprised to discover that I lapped it all up. Doors had been opened for me to a completely new world.

Despite the late night, I woke up early on the Saturday morning and left Freddie sleeping. I went into the kitchen, made myself a cup of coffee and gazed out of the bedroom window. Eventually the flat started to stir. Freddie got up in the middle of the morning and Joe went out to buy some provisions. For the first time on that trip Freddie and I were together, alone. We cuddled on the sofa, talking about anything which came into our heads. Before we knew it, the day had flown by.

After supper, we ventured out to the pubs and clubs. I discovered that I had become known as the mystery man on Freddie Mercury's arm. Most of Munich's gay society were wondering who the hell I was. Freddie would only introduce me as 'My new man'. We laughed and danced all night before falling back into bed.

The next day, Sunday, I had to leave for London at the end of the afternoon. I was very sorry to say goodbye to Freddie. As a friend drove me to the airport, I started getting myself ready to return to my quiet, modest life in Sutton and devote myself to the daily routine of the Savoy barber's shop. I was thrilled about the weekend with Freddie but didn't dare tell a soul where I'd been. I simply carried on with the haircuts ahead of me, happy inside to have found Freddie.

I wrote to thank him for the wonderful weekend and included a picture of a big ginger tom cat called Spock I used to have. I was thrilled when Freddie rang during the week.

The next weekend I was back on my own in London. On Saturday night I headed back to the Market Tavern for a few beers. On Sunday I treated myself to a lie-in, then tackled Mrs Taverner's garden, which I enjoyed. Gardening has always been a joy for me and I could dig and prune all day.

One of the lines from Freddie's song 'I Was Born to Love You' was: 'It's so hard to believe this is happening to me, an amazing feeling coming through.' That summed up just how I felt about my affair with Freddie. The next time I saw Freddie was when he invited me to watch the making of the video for that very song at a studio in the East End of London. In the video, two Dutch dancers were doing a sultry bar-room routine of a Frenchman and his sexy partner. Late into the evening disaster struck. The Frenchman threw his girl across the stage but she slipped and smashed her head. Freddie stopped everything and took her to hospital, where he waited in the corridor while she was examined. Even though it was late at night, Freddie's visit caused a stir and soon he was signing autographs for excited young nurses and insomniac elderly patients.

The following Friday an air ticket was again waiting to fly me to Munich for the weekend and, very nearly, my first fight with Freddie. This time I declined his generous offer of a chauffeur to drive me to Heathrow. It all seemed a bit daft: he had to drive from West London to the West End then back out to Heathrow. I got the Tube instead. Again I was flying first-class.

Joe met me at the airport, but Freddie wasn't with him. Joe said he had some long-standing engagement. Joe usually knew every single move Freddie made – he was told everything – but that night he said he didn't have a clue where Freddie was. He wasn't even sure that Freddie would be home that night.

On Freddie's instructions, Joe took me to the Bermuda Triangle bars and we ended up again in New York New York. When he decided he'd had enough and wanted to go home, I still wanted to stay. So he left me in the capable hands of another 'Family' member, a fellow Irishman called Patrick.

When New York New York closed I went to Patrick's flat for a drink and then he walked me back to Freddie's. Freddie had made it home by then and, I thought, was sound asleep. I quietly undressed, got into bed and cuddled up.

'Where have you been to at this hour in the morning?' he snapped.

'Out with Patrick,' I answered.

He remained silent all night. The following morning we didn't say a word to each other for hours. Finally, Freddie broke the ice and apologised for not having been at the airport when I arrived.

I'm not sure why, but I had the distinct impression that Freddie had another boyfriend in the city somewhere. I thought back to my arrival a fortnight earlier and realised why Freddie probably wanted me there so desperately. I was just part of a game between lovers. He wanted to flaunt me so that his boyfriend would see or hear of me and be jealous. Freddie had managed it all very successfully.

Again that night Freddie and the Family ended up in New York New York. There I caught a glimpse of the opposition. A German boy was pointed out to me by Barbara as Freddie's lover. He was quite different from me in many ways. Freddie liked his boyfriends fairly big; you could say he was a bit of a 'chubby chaser'. Although this guy, called Winnie Kirkenberger, was fairly plump – perhaps because he owned a restaurant – and like me he had dark hair and moustache, unlike me he looked very aggressive.

Whenever Winnie appeared Freddie made a big fuss of me, while the dark German shot me piercing glances. Back home with Freddie that night I was tempted to tell him I wasn't prepared to be a pawn in his game. But, as we got into bed, I decided to say nothing.

The next day, Sunday, we pottered around the flat, cuddling on the sofa and watching telly. Then I flew home and, over the next fortnight, wrote to Freddie a number of times. He was now a large part of my life.

The next weekend Freddie came back to London and introduced me for the first time to Mary Austin, a petite woman with shoulder-length fair hair, blue eyes and a fair complexion. Mary was reserved but very welcoming when we met. She worked as company secretary of Freddie's private company, Goose Productions, which managed all Freddie's personal affairs and paid his staff. Mary lived and worked about a hundred yards away in a flat owned either by Freddie or by his company.

The following weekend, now well into a routine, I flew to Germany. A car met me and when I got to the flat Freddie was waiting to greet me. Then he slapped me in the eye: he said he was going with Winnie, out of Munich, up in the 'Hills of Bavaria' – and off he went. He didn't come home at all that night. I didn't let any of this upset me. Perhaps I was a little naive. I hoped the two of them were just tying up the loose ends of their failed love affair.

The next morning the phone rang and it was Freddie, inviting me and Joe to meet him at Winnie's place above his restaurant. We strolled through the city to Winnie's flat and let ourselves in. Freddie breezed by and trilled: 'Right, let's go.'

We strolled back the way we had come and dived into a pet shop where we fell in love with the kittens. Freddie bought tins and tins of cat food, in flavours you couldn't buy in London, as well as little toys for his beloved Tiffany and Oscar.

When we came out of the shop it happened. As we were crossing the main street, Freddie leaped up into my arms. If I hadn't caught him he'd have crashed to the ground. He smothered me in wet kisses, and I was so embarrassed that I dropped him and ran off. He made a few more runs at me before he left me alone. I couldn't handle this sort of thing in public, so I kept well ahead of him.

We went back to the flat and Freddie was desperate to jump into bed for sex. His drive was amazing. Then we flaked out on the sofa, watching television. It was something we did an awful lot in our time together alone. On the sofa Freddie and I usually sat side by side. Sometimes he'd lie one way and me the other, and I'd massage his feet. He adored that. We rarely drank anything stronger than water or tea in the daytime, though we quickly made amends each evening.

Freddie loved old black-and-white movies and the early Technicolor classics – stuff from the Bette Davis era. He also liked old comedies, such as *Some Like It Hot* and *The Women*. But his favourite was the Marx Brothers; he was a great fan of theirs, as the titles of the two Queen albums, *A Day at the Races* and *A Night at the Opera*, prove. In fact, the band had to seek permission from Groucho Marx to use the titles. Freddie told me his response had been warm-hearted and, as you'd expect, very witty. He replied: 'I am very pleased you have named one of your albums after my film and that you are being successful. I would be very happy for you to call your next one after my latest film, *The Greatest Hits of the Rolling Stones*!'

The following weekend, back at Stafford Terrace, Freddie was to reveal an unlikely secret. After breakfast on Sunday, several of his friends arrived – including Trevor 'BB' Clarke, a caterer; an artist called Rudi Patterson; and Mary Austin with Joe Bert, her musician boyfriend, formerly with Tom Robinson's band Sector 27.

'We're going for a walk,' Freddie announced to us. It was gloriously sunny and we strolled for about twenty minutes – about half a mile – until we came to a gate in a long wall. Freddie unlocked it and led us through into a magical secret garden.

Garden Lodge, 1 Logan Place, is a large Georgian house

set inside a large, mature English garden behind high brick walls.

Freddie had bought the place at the end of the seventies from the Hoare banking family – hence its nickname under Freddie's ownership: the Hoare House. He had gutted it, totally renovating and redecorating it just the way he wanted. That Sunday the last of the builders and decorators were about to move out; the place was almost ready for Freddie to move into.

The front door of Garden Lodge leads into a large, light hallway with an elegant wide staircase. To the left and right, double doors lead to two spectacularly spacious rooms, parquet-floored with expansive windows gazing out over the garden. The room to the right was the most magnificent, a massive space with a minstrels' gallery and tall windows. It had once been an artist's studio, hence the windows. Behind this room were the kitchen and dining room.

Upstairs, several rooms had been knocked into one to give Freddie a large master bedroom suite. From the landing you first entered a dressing room with a large plaster dome. On either side was a bathroom, each finished in Italian marble with gold fittings. The room on the left, decorated in veined white, grey and pink marble, boasted a jacuzzi bath big enough for three. The sleek bathroom on the right was decorated in black panels. Ahead were the large sliding double doors, which always remained open, leading to the bedroom. The walls were in a pinkish cream colour moiré – water-marked fabric. Straight ahead were large windows opening on to a long balcony, and to the right a window which looked straight on to the garden. Freddie's Queen-size bed was to the left of the room.

The jewel of the house was undoubtedly the garden, which made the house totally private. We spent most of that first visit outside, sitting on a small mound, soaking up the sun and larking around.

Freddie had mentioned Garden Lodge in passing, but the house was far more magnificent than I'd expected. But at that time, however beautiful the London house, Freddie still thought of Germany as his main home.

Freddie would work on Queen albums in both London and Munich, and it was during one of what were to be many sessions that I met the members of the band for the first time: guitarist Brian May, drummer Roger Taylor and bassist John Deacon. They were immediately very friendly and struck me as down-to-earth. Roger had run a stall at Kensington Market with Freddie years earlier and they were clearly soulmates; they'd often sit together, giggling. Brian was very intellectual and meticulous about his music. But it was John Deacon I took to most. He was the silent member of the group – remarkably modest, quiet and unassuming. He and Freddie were the most closely involved in the business side of Queen when they started out, and John had doubled as the band's accountant. Later, their success wildly escalated the demands of the job. His running gag was: 'I'm only the bass player.'

The next big event was Freddie releasing his new solo single, 'Made in Heaven'. The video for the track was an incredible production, with a Dante's *Inferno* theme boasting a 60-foot rotating globe, apocalyptic fires, raging storms and a ton of extras.

Freddie invited me to visit the set after work, but I didn't reckon on the reception I'd get. I went up to the security guy on the studio gate and asked for Freddie's trailer. He pointed it out and I ambled over.

When I opened the door, Freddie was very jumpy.

'How did you get here?' he snapped. Then he flew into a rage, insisting that security had to be made much tighter.

When he calmed down, he told me why he was so jittery. Some time before, a man had broken into Freddie's flat and tried on all of his clothes. He had been caught by the police and put behind bars, but the incident had upset Freddie enormously.

The morning of the video shoot Freddie learned that the man had escaped from prison; his girlfriend had alerted the police that her man was out, armed, dangerous and probably looking for Freddie Mercury. The police were taking the threat so seriously that they had sealed off both entrances to his house in Stafford Terrace. After a while the drama passed; the poor man was caught by the police and put back in prison where he belonged.

Filming the video lasted late into the night, and when we got back to Freddie's flat around five in the morning a couple of policemen were waiting for us. They said they wanted to make sure Freddie was feeling all right after his ordeal, and they stayed and joked for a while.

And Freddie joked back.

He pointed to a little antique Japanese lacquered box.

'I suppose you're wondering what's in that box, aren't you?' he said. 'It's my drugs!'

They burst out laughing.

After they'd gone, by which time it was about six, Freddie said to me: 'You go and have an hour's lie-down. I'll wake you for work, don't worry.'

An hour later Freddie woke me, softly, saying: 'You'd better be getting off to work, darling. I've run the bath.'

2

MAKE YOUR MIND UP

Back at the Savoy a week or so later I received an internal call from a woman asking to make an appointment for a Mr Jones. She wanted it to be as late as possible, which was 5.30pm.

I would always allow clients to be ten minutes late, but when, at 5.40pm, there was still no sign of Mr Jones I rang and asked to be put through to his room. The woman who'd made the appointment answered and I created merry hell over her man being late.

'We close soon. We close at six o'clock,' I said. 'He'll have to come down now.' A few minutes later he arrived: it was David Bowie. I didn't recognise Freddie when I first met him, but I recognised Bowie at once. As Ziggy Stardust he'd triggered off a whole style era a decade earlier – a trend for Bowie haircuts, of which I'd done my fair share.

When I finished cutting his hair, I asked: 'You are who I think you are, aren't you?'

'Who do you think I am?' he asked back.

'David Bowie,' I said.

'Yes,' he said.

And that was the only conversation we had.

The next Saturday, 13 July 1985, was a sweltering hot day – set to be a very special day for Freddie and me. After finishing work at the Savoy I made my way to his flat. The place was buzzing. Freddie was in party mood.

Everyone was absorbed in watching *Live Aid* on television.

At about four in the afternoon Freddie turned to me and asked: 'Aren't you going to get ready, then?' I was still in my suit straight from work.

'What for?' I asked.

'We're going to *Live Aid*!' he screamed, and my mouth fell to the floor. I'd never been to a concert before, a fact that Freddie didn't know.

'I've got nothing to wear,' I spluttered.

'You don't need anything,' he replied. 'Just get your jeans on and there are T-shirts in the wardrobe. Help yourself.'

We swept to Wembley in the back of one of a fleet of black limousines. I was on my way to see Queen perform live on stage for the very first time. We arrived at Wembley with about an hour to spare. The special enclosure was awash with the country's greatest rock performers. I was agog.

Each member of the band had his own dressing room trailer and all three wives were there – Chrissy May, Dominique Taylor and Veronica Deacon, as well as the May and Taylor children.

To be behind the scenes at Wembley that day was incredible: the atmosphere was electric. Freddie knew everyone: Paul McCartney, Status Quo, Sting, U2, Dire Straits. When we found Elton John I was introduced by Freddie as 'My new man'. Phil Collins came up and asked for Freddie's autograph.

'For you?' asked Freddie.

'No,' said Phil. 'It's for my kids.' Freddie laughed and signed.

He went to get ready. Queen would be appearing after David Bowie, who was on stage now. Freddie was going on in what he was wearing – jeans, white vest, studded amulet and belt.

When David Bowie came off and headed into his own trailer, Freddie whisked after him, taking me with him. David was strange. He was sitting wet through in front of an electric fan, trying to dry his hair.

'It's about the only fan you've got, David, isn't it?' quipped Freddie. They laughed. Then Freddie said: 'This is Jim. I believe you've already met.'

David glanced up at me and looked blank: 'No, I don't know him at all.'

'Well, who did your hair the other night?' I said, but I don't think it registered. Very strange.

When it was time for Queen to go on, I walked with Freddie to the stage and, watching from the wings, witnessed the most magical twenty minutes of my life. The group tore into 'Hammer to Fall', 'Crazy Little Thing Called Love', 'Bohemian Rhapsody', 'Radio GaGa' and 'We Are the Champions'. (Later Freddie and Brian performed the moving Queen song 'Is This the World We Created', with all royalties going to the Save The Children Fund.)

At last I had seen the real Freddie Mercury at work, whipping seventy thousand people into a frenzy. He gave everything to his performance; nothing else mattered to him. When he came off, he rushed to his trailer and I tottered behind like a puppy. His first words were: 'Thank God that's over!' Joe ripped his wet clothes from him and dressed him. Adrenalin still overflowing, Freddie knocked back a large vodka to calm himself. Then his face lit up. The expression said: 'Yes, we've done it!'

As we stepped out of the caravan we met a grinning Elton John. 'You bastards!' he said to Freddie. 'You stole the show!' Then they hugged. Everyone backstage was converging on Freddie, Brian, Roger and John. Organiser Bob Geldof said later: 'Queen were simply the best band of the day.'

We stayed until the end of the show and met George Michael, but ducked the after-show party to celebrate at home and watch the American end of the amazing concert on television.

When Phil Collins popped up in Philadelphia's JFK Stadium, having opened Wembley and then dashed over the

Atlantic by Concorde, Freddie shook his head in amazement. 'Doesn't that man ever stop?' he asked.

We sat around drinking, mulling over all the performances. Freddie's favourites were Tina Turner and Mick Jagger singing 'Private Dancer'.

When we fell into bed that night, Freddie cuddled up and whispered: 'Did you enjoy it?'

'What do you think?' I answered, hugging him tight. 'It's the first time I've ever been to a concert.'

'You're joking!' he said.

'No,' I added. He was dumbfounded. I fell asleep knowing that for the first time I'd actually seen the real star Freddie Mercury doing what he did best – wowing the world.

The next morning *Live Aid* seemed an age away to Freddie, but not to me. When I got to the Savoy on Monday morning it was still bursting out of my ears.

I was soon back in the old routine. Every two weeks I would fly to Munich and be met at the airport. The first time after *Live Aid* I flew to Munich to join Freddie I was whisked direct to the Musicland studio, to watch him working on material for Queen's new album, *A Kind of Magic*, which included tracks for the film *Highlander*. The spacious basement studio was on the outskirts of the city under a massive complex of flats which Joe nicknamed 'Suicide Block'. Its best claim to fame was that Giorgio Moroder had written and recorded most of his greatest disco hits there.

Freddie took me to the control room and introduced me to Reinhold Mack, his German producer. He was a tall, thin man in his late thirties – he looked like an ageing hippy and had shoulder-length hair. Freddie sat me down and disappeared to carry on recording.

In the studio Freddie had a one-track mind – work, work and more work. I watched him through the glass, but he rarely glanced my way because he was so totally absorbed in his work. He chain-smoked or, rather, chain-lit Silk Cuts, and to boost his energy and adrenalin he slipped down slugs of Russian vodka. He only drank Stolichnaya.

Freddie's sense of drive amazed me. He had to keep on the go; it was part of his life blood. When he wasn't singing he'd bounce into the control room and sit behind the banks of sliders to tweak the playback mixes himself. He was always in total control. At the end of a session I might mention that I liked this or that about a song, but I never knew if he took any notice of what I thought.

Freddie worked until about eleven that night before calling it a day. We set off to a club in the Bermuda Triangle before heading home. Next day Freddie wanted to go back into the studio to work. As I was to learn, he had a habit of passing the studio saying he would 'just pop in for five or six minutes', but then stay five or six hours.

Some weekends Freddie would beaver away alone; often he would work with Brian, Roger and John. When the other members of Queen were in Munich to record, they would stay in a hotel. In the studio, the boys liked to have their own teams around them to do odd chores, like making tea or coffee. Freddie had his two assistants, Phoebe and Joe; Brian had Jobby; and Roger had Chris 'Crystal' Taylor. In one corner of the studio there was an exercise bike which was in use from time to time whenever the going got slow.

At the end of a session, the whole group would break off and we'd head off to eat together. We'd find a modest pavement café or restaurant nearby and have a simple lunch or supper.

After hours working on the same track, the band developed a way of diffusing the tension of their work: they swapped the real lyrics for funnier send-up lines. Those off-the-record versions of Queen hits were always hysterically funny, and the whole studio would erupt in laughter.

One night the band recorded one of the tracks destined for *Highlander*, 'One Vision'. It came out as 'Fried Chicken'! Later that night, when I was alone with Freddie, I said to him: 'Come on, for Christ's sake! The band is big enough. You're bold enough.'

'For what?' he asked.

'To put that line in. Fried Chicken!'

He said nothing.

Whenever Freddie came back to London he stayed at Garden Lodge. One weekend there in August we talked about what kind of party he should stage for his thirty-ninth birthday, on 5 September. I suggested that he should have a black-and-white party and he seemed to like the idea. Typically, Freddie transformed it into an outrageous and amazing event, a black-and-white drag ball.

He took over Henderson's, a top nightclub in Munich. Then he had it redecorated and refurbished throughout in black and white and decorated with hundreds of black and white roses. Even the seats were re-covered in black and white. The ball was to be recorded for the video of his solo single, 'Living on My Own', released that month.

On the day of the party a load of us were flown in from London, including Phoebe, Mary, some of the Queen office workers and *Daily Express* showbusiness writer David Wigg. David and Queen had known each other for over ten years: he was one of the few writers whom Freddie felt he could trust.

Going through British customs there was a bit of a hold-up. We were bringing with us Freddie's costume for the ball, which included a pair of braces decorated with mock bullets. The airline decided that the bullet braces couldn't be allowed in the cabin and had to be put in the cargo hold.

We flew British Airways. As the only one travelling business-class, I had free drinks and better food than the others. Mary suggested that I steal a bottle of wine from business-class and pass it back to them. I did nothing of the sort. It would have been too tacky.

Most of the party were put up at the Munich Hilton Hotel at Freddie's expense, but Mary was staying with Freddie and me, sleeping on the sofabed in his apartment. By the time Mary and I arrived there was a houseful of guests.

My heart sank when I got to the flat and saw all the

expensive birthday presents that Freddie's friends had provided. I hadn't been sure what to give him. I didn't have much money to buy him anything, so I decided I'd give him a pressed four-leaf clover. It wasn't a real one, of course, but it had been given to me many years ago by a friend's father who had made it himself.

I was too embarrassed to give Freddie his lucky clover in front of everyone, so I called him into the bedroom.

'I'm sorry, this is all I can afford to give you,' I said, passing him a small folded piece of tissue paper. When he opened it up he was thrilled. He kissed me then ran into the sitting room with it.

'Look at the gorgeous present Jim's given me,' he told everyone, and I blushed. Freddie seemed delighted with it because he knew I had given him something from the heart.

At about ten, Freddie and I set off for the party in the limousine. Freddie was wearing his black-and-white harlequin leotard and a wonderful military-style braided jacket designed by the Emanuels, the designers who had made Lady Di's celebrated wedding dress. And of course he wore the bullet braces which had caused the trouble at the airport. Everyone was dressed in black and white or drag that night – except me. I was in a multi-coloured sequined jacket with tails, borrowed from a former dancer friend. As I was wearing black trousers I argued that I could get away with it – and I did.

Most of the crowd at the bash were German, familiar faces on the Munich gay scene who'd go anywhere for a good party. Some of the costumes were ingenious. Brian May came as a witch; David Wigg wore a fetching frock; Phoebe went as a gypsy; and even Richard Young, a paparazzi photographer, was dragged up to the nines. Reinhold Mack was there with his wife, Ingrid, and so was Steve Strange as well as a number of record company bosses.

Film cameras slipped among us constantly, catching the magic. I spent most of my time around Freddie, but wanted to maintain my anonymity, so whenever the cameras were around I'd make myself scarce. I became quite adept at slipping into the shadows at the first sign of a lens.

During the evening Freddie was presented with an enormous birthday cake in the shape of a grand piano. It was so large that each of the three hundred guests got a slice.

Some hours into the party Joe came to me looking worried. 'Freddie wants you,' he said, then went on to explain that Freddie was having some kind of anxiety attack. I found him in the middle of the room, looking totally exhausted. He'd had an argument with someone – who it was and what it was about I've no idea. By the time I arrived the drama was over. Freddie wanted me to help him calm down, so I put my arms around him and hugged him. I soon discovered it wasn't only the argument which had got him into such a state.

All there was to drink that night was champagne, champagne and more champagne. We'd all had a few, but Freddie had had more than he'd bargained for. Drugs were going around and someone had slipped him some kind of drugs cocktail. Although he liked cocaine, he didn't like experimenting with different drugs. He was quite shattered by the experience.

After a while Freddie felt fine again. We partied on into the night and even went on to the dance floor. It was a night to remember, and we finally crashed into bed at six in the morning. While most of us took the day slowly, the following morning Freddie went back to the club with the video crew and some darling German drag queens, slender stunners, to film more footage of his outrageous video.

When Freddie got the bill for the party he wasn't too amused. The cost was enormous, about £50,000, because so many people had been extravagant at his expense. He felt he had been taken for a ride.

When the video came out, to my amazement I was included for a brief moment, dancing alone with my shirt off. Freddie was so meticulous about the editing of his videos that he must have insisted I should be included. The video was never released in America because CBS, Freddie's solo label, believed it was too risqué: there was too much transvestism in it for them.

By those happy days the relationship between Freddie and me had deepened. I came to miss him when we were apart; I became upset. And Freddie felt the same way about me. Then one weekend in London he started talking about living our lives together.

'If I asked you to come and live with me in Munich, would you?' he asked. I'd never even considered moving in with Freddie until that moment.

'Yes, I will,' I said, adding, 'on one condition. If I move to Germany I must have a job.' I had financial commitments in Britain, and wasn't prepared to throw in my job at the Savoy to scour Munich for a job as a hairdresser who couldn't even speak German. My independence was terribly important to me, and I wasn't prepared simply to live out of Freddie's pocket.

Freddie let the matter drop. Then, fifteen minutes later, he said: 'And if I later decide to leave Munich and come back to London?'

'Then I would consider what I wanted to do,' I answered. It was that independent streak in me which caused most of the rows between us, always ending in Freddie screaming: 'You and your fucking independence!' In fact, Freddie adored independent-minded people, but he preferred to manipulate people into doing what he wanted if he could.

I was never in any doubt that it was he who engineered the love affair between us. It happened like this. One night in London we went to the Earls Court gay club Copacabana with Joe, Peter Straker and Gary, the chauffeur, among others. We headed to the bar, then strolled towards the pool table. Suddenly Freddie turned and stared at me.

'Fuck off!' he said venomously. I was very surprised. So I did. I fucked off. I turned on my heel and made for the door. On the way out I passed Gary, who sensed that all was not well.

'What's happened?' he asked.

'I don't know,' I said. 'He's in one of his moods and has told me to fuck off, so I'm going.' I walked back to Garden Lodge, packed my weekend bag and took a taxi to Trafalgar Square to catch the night bus back to Sutton. I got home, went to bed and fell asleep. At four in the morning I was woken by a furious Ivy Taverner banging on my bedroom door. Unable to reach me in any other way, Freddie had telephoned Ivy and she'd slammed the phone down on him. I apologised to her, but it didn't seem to help.

I was at least as stubborn as Freddie and had no intention of calling him the next morning. When he did ring, a few days later, I blew him out. 'Don't fuck me around,' I told him. 'Nobody tells me to fuck off.'

He knew things weren't over between us. Far from it; the fatal late night phone calls were about to start.

For the next few weeks he took to phoning most nights at three or four in the morning. Eventually Ivy Taverner got so fed up with it that she gave me two weeks' notice. Freddie's persistence had made me homeless.

When Freddie came back to London I told him I was being evicted. 'I'm being kicked out because of your late night calls,' I said.

'Well, don't worry about it,' he said calmly. 'Move into Garden Lodge. There's no one there – it's empty.' So I did.

After two years living in Germany Freddie decided he'd had enough of being a tax exile, sticking to a limited number of days he could spend in Britain every year. He wanted to come back to London and take up residence at Garden Lodge. For the time being he planned to keep his flat in Stafford Terrace and move things across to the house slowly over several months.

When I arrived at Garden Lodge, we were not quite alone, Phoebe was already living there, with the cats Tiffany and Oscar. But Freddie's plans to come back from Munich to London to be with me for my first weekend at Garden Lodge were scuppered.

I packed a few bags at Sutton and was just setting off

when Mary asked me to call on her. She told me Freddie was snowed in in Munich; he would not be joining me quite so soon. Then she handed me a note that Freddie had written a week or two earlier to deliver to me.

I still have the small Japanese card Freddie had written: 'Take lots of care, will see you soon. Tons of love F.'

So I spent my first night in the large master bedroom alone, with Oscar snuggling up on top of the massive bed. I hung up a few shirts and my suit for work, but otherwise I didn't unpack – I didn't know where to put my things. Freddie arrived the following weekend and immediately dragged me off to bed. He said he had missed me terribly; I knew he meant it. After he had picked out wardrobes for me to use in the dressing area, he cleared all his things from one of his drawers.

'That's for your little bits and pieces,' he said.

So that's how I came to move in with him. We lived together for the next six years like man and wife.

Freddie played the groom when he took part in *FashionAid*, the Live Aid fashion show at the Royal Albert Hall in November. Just like the concert, this was a glittering affair with celebrities by the score. Freddie was wearing the jacket he'd worn at his Munich birthday party, but with black trousers. His partner was the actress Jane Seymour. She was modelling a sensational white wedding dress, also designed by the Emanuels. Others who went ahead of them on the catwalk included Boy George and Julie Goodyear, star of the soap *Coronation Street*; *Dempsey and Makepeace* couple Michael Brandon and Glynis Barber; Alison Moyet; Shirley Bassey; Lenny Henry; George Michael and his Wham! partner Andrew Ridgeley; and newly dubbed 'Saint' Bob Geldof and Paula Yates.

The after-show party was held at the Hyde Park Hotel. Freddie and Jane arrived in their outfits and brought the foyer to a standstill. The place was packed with American tourists who thought the couple were for real. Jane was a big Hollywood name and they recognised her at once.

When they discovered her new 'husband' was Freddie it seemed so unlikely that they must have thought they were witnessing a real scoop of a story. They even applauded and took photographs.

Like any other couple, Freddie and I got around to the question of the housekeeping money. Thankfully, given Freddie's ability to spend money like water, I wasn't the main breadwinner in the family. But we agreed that it was only fair to share the running costs and settled on me paying him a weekly allowance of £50. It represented over half my weekly wage although Freddie never knew that. But I paid it willingly; it went some way to keeping our relationship on a fair footing but later he dropped the idea.

That same month there was a pleasant surprise for me when Queen released their single 'One Vision'. The final line to the song had been changed to 'Just gimme, gimme, gimme *fried chicken*!' just as I had suggested.

The video for 'One Vision' was filmed in Musicland by two gentlemen always referred to affectionately as the Torpedo Twins – director and producer duo Rudi Dolezal and Hans Rossacher. Both were tall, big Austrians. Rudi wore more colourful clothes than his partner, but they were equally jovial and friendly.

As Christmas approached, 'One Vision' quickly climbed the charts, and the success put an extra bounce into Freddie's step. There was no new album for their fans that year, so Queen released *The Complete Works*, a limited edition boxed set of eleven of their albums. I'm afraid it was probably out of the reach of most fans' pockets.

A more popular move was the band's ambitious decision to mount a tour of Europe the following summer. The man who put Queen's tours together was already on the case: he was Gerry Stickles and I met him one day when he came to Garden Lodge for a meeting. Gerry was the daddy of them all – a plump American in his forties. I took to him enormously. He was a bit of a comedian and had an endless supply of very funny jokes.

What present to give Freddie for Christmas took lots of thought. What do you give a man who has everything? In the end my friend John Rowell came up with the answer. John was a very personable man, the same height and age as me but much slimmer, and he ran Key Largo, a clothes shop in Covent Garden where I'd bought a leather jacket. It had cost me a small fortune at the time – about £200. Freddie admired it a great deal, so John arranged for me to buy a similar jacket for Freddie for Christmas, paying him in instalments.

Then, a fortnight before Christmas, Freddie and I had a flaming row over a stocky little guy nicknamed Danish Bacon. He was from south London somewhere. Freddie would always flirt terribly with other gay men when we went out, but I didn't worry; I knew I was the one he'd end up in bed with later. I instinctively knew he had messed around with other men a number of times before and it made me feel terribly jealous, though not possessive. That night when he flirted with Danish Bacon I decided I'd had enough.

I dragged Freddie up to the bedroom in Garden Lodge and confronted him about it. I told him he had to make his mind up about what he wanted – me or another guy. Then I walked out.

I phoned John Rowell, who lived between Vauxhall and Clapham in south London, to explain the situation and he instantly offered me his spare room. I packed enough clothes for work and left Garden Lodge. If Freddie wanted to play the field, I wasn't going to get in his way.

A few days later, Freddie rang me at work. He asked me to go to Garden Lodge when I had finished at the Savoy to talk things over.

'I'm sorry about what's happened,' he said. 'Come on home.' So we kissed and made up. I moved back in the week before Christmas and found myself frantically running around buying presents for Freddie's inner circle. I could hardly afford to buy any, as I'd spent so much on Freddie's jacket.

That first Christmas at Garden Lodge we had a decorated tree in the lounge, but for some reason we didn't get round to decorating the rest of the house. On Christmas Eve we went to Heaven and got home legless in the early hours. When Freddie and I woke up together for our first Christmas morning, we kissed and said 'Happy Christmas'. We got up and headed downstairs to get everything ready for lunch with a handful of close friends – Joe and Phoebe, Trevor Clarke, Mary and Peter Straker.

Ten of us sat down to roast turkey, pork and ham that first year. We pulled crackers, donned crêpe paper hats and tucked into the feast. Three hours later, we settled down in front of the Christmas tree to open our presents. Someone dived into the mountain under the tree and threw presents out in all directions. Freddie got up himself to find his present for me and brought it over. Then I found my present for him.

Freddie gave me a Cartier lighter. And with his Christmas card to me was a cheque. My eyes popped out of my head. It was for £1000. I was astounded.

Freddie gave everyone close to him a Christmas present and a cheque with which to buy something they really liked. It was his way of thanking everyone for all the hard work they had put in over the year. He gave everyone the same amount except Mary, who would perhaps receive a little more.

When I gave Freddie my present he immediately tried it on. It fitted perfectly. But, while he was clearly pleased at the time, he didn't really like it. He only wore it once more.

That day I got to know Peter Straker a lot better. He became one of Freddie's closest friends, until it all ended in tears. At earlier meetings I couldn't work out what to make of Peter but I soon took to him. I decided I liked him and I think he liked me. Phoebe, however, loathed him.

Peter Straker was one of the few people guaranteed always to make Freddie laugh. He was a singer, which meant that, like Freddie, he rarely had to get up early in the morning. That gave them the excuse to stay up together all night long, watching videos and listening to music. They both shared a great love of gospel music, but could never manage to listen to it quietly while the rest of us were asleep.

On Boxing Day Garden Lodge played host to thirty friends. Freddie's hospitality, like his festive spirit, flowed freely. Then New Year's Eve there was another party to which I invited my ex-boyfriend John Alexander. He knew no one, so I found myself spending a lot of my time keeping him company. On the stroke of midnight we ran around in all directions wishing each other Happy New Year and kissing one another. I was saddened to see that, rather pointedly, the only person Freddie didn't wish a Happy New Year was John. I said nothing.

Most of us moved on to Heaven. John came along, too, and once inside the club drifted away from the group. A little later I realised I hadn't seen Freddie for a while. I took a look around, but there was no sign of him. Then I asked Joe if he had seen Freddie.

'On the dance floor,' he said. There I noticed Freddie dancing with a guy I didn't know. I just watched for a while. Then I saw that Freddie was going a bit far with his dancing partner. I watched a little longer until I could bear it no more and staggered into action. I stumbled my way across the packed floor and grabbed Freddie.

'I want a word with you,' I yelled at him, whisking him towards the wall. His new-found friend, who I later learned was called George, started to follow, but I swung around and threatened him. 'You keep your fucking nose out of this,' I growled.

I pinned Freddie into a corner with my arm around his neck. I spat at him: 'Don't, on New Year's morning, fuck around with me.'

'All right, let go,' he said. 'I've got what I wanted. I just wanted you to show you're jealous.'

I let go of him and he marched off. I stayed put and finished my drink.

When I went to find the others, they were nowhere to be found. They'd left the club – and left me in a right pickle. It was freezing cold outside and I was just wearing jeans and a singlet. What is worse, my jacket and house-keys were in the car they had gone home in. I was furious. It was New Year's Day and it would be impossible to find a cab anywhere.

It must have been about five in the morning when I finally got back to Garden Lodge. I pressed the bell and heard Peter Straker's voice through the intercom speaker saying, 'It's Jim!'

He pressed the gate-lock button and as I walked up the garden path Freddie came out. I began screaming and shouting and went straight upstairs to our bedroom. Freddie ran after me.

'Look,' I said, 'you make your mind up. You want me or you want somebody else? Just make your mind up.'

And I didn't leave things there. I took Freddie to task for snubbing John: 'How dare you insult my friends like that!'

Freddie pinned me on to the bed to try to calm me down. It didn't take long for me to cheer up. He gave me a winning look which said 'I'm sorry', though I never actually heard him say those words to anyone.

'I got the reaction out of you tonight that I've always wanted from you,' he said and slung his arms around me. I squeezed him tight around the waist. We made up properly in the bedroom later when we finally booted out the last few New Year's revellers.

Next day I got up and brought Freddie an early morning cup of tea. It was business as usual.

Three days later it was my thirty-seventh birthday. Freddie decided to give me two new suits and asked Joe to take me shopping in Savile Row. The first suit I bought was a Tommy Nutter, and a sharp contrast with the off-the-peg suits I was used to.

But Freddie's plan to throw a birthday party for me at Garden Lodge quickly led the two of us to blows. It was a great party and brought together my friends and Freddie's for the first time. The birthday cake was a triumph. It was decorated with cat figures, which I then kept in the fridge for over two years.

But a few days later Freddie accused one of my friends of stealing a small, quite valuable vase from the windowsill in the hallway. I was adamant that I knew my friends very well and that none of them would do such a thing. For weeks the same argument kept coming back. Whenever we were alone in the bedroom, Freddie would niggle away, saying: 'Someone stole the vase. You and your bloody friends. They're never coming here again.'

Finally I snapped. 'Fine, Freddie,' I said. 'I'm going to the homes of all of my friends and if I find the vase I will leave you. You'll never hear from me again.'

After a while he lightened up. 'It's only a vase, anyway,' he said.

Only after Freddie had died did I finally learn the truth about the missing vase. Joe told me it had been broken on the day of the party, before a single guest had arrived. To prevent Freddie hearing about the breakage, Joe buried the broken pieces amongst the rubbish in the dustbin.

'Why didn't you tell Freddie at the time to save all that hassle?' I asked.

'We thought it best if Freddie thought it had been stolen rather than broken,' Joe replied.

That said a lot about Freddie. He loved beautiful things.

3

A RARE DECEIT

February the 14th 1986 was our first Valentine's Day together. I ordered two dozen red roses for 'FM' to be delivered to Garden Lodge in the morning while I was at work. But Freddie turned the romantic tables on me. The hotel's florist came into the barber's shop around noon with a beautiful bouquet of two dozen red roses.

Maria, my assistant, screamed out in delight: 'Oh, they're for me.' But hers wasn't the only face which fell to the floor as the florist explained: 'No, in actual fact they're for Jim!' The customer in my chair looked on in amazement as I went bright scarlet with embarrassment. I opened the card and it simply read 'F'.

Freddie's friend Dave Clark, the drumming star of the sixties group the Dave Clark Five, was staging *Time*, a rock musical, at the Dominion Theatre, starring Cliff Richard and a hologram of Laurence Olivier. Dave asked Freddie to write two songs for the show, one of them the title song, 'Time'.

The show was due to open on 9 April and Freddie was invited to the celebrity opening night. He wanted me to go with him. Weeks ahead of the night, Joe was asked to buy smart black dinner suits and shiny patent leather shoes for himself, Phoebe and me.

Ironically, the opening line of Freddie's centrepiece song 'Time' was 'Time waits for no man'. But time almost ran out between Freddie and me before we even got to that opening night. I discovered he was being unfaithful again. While I'd be at home most nights, content to watch television and get to bed early, Freddie continued going out alone until late. Some nights he went out and never came home at all. His excuse was that he'd stayed over at Stafford Terrace. I heard different. Friends whispered they'd seen Freddie openly playing the field.

I was aware that Joe always knew where Freddie was. I woke up one Sunday morning at about nine. Freddie had, as usual, stayed out the whole night. When Joe came down he made straight for the door, and I followed at a safe distance. He led me to Freddie, who was, exactly as he had said, in the flat in Stafford Terrace.

Joe went in through the front door and, about twenty minutes later, re-emerged with Freddie. But then I noticed a third person, a young guy, slipping out of the door and off down the road. I concluded that the gossip about Freddie was true.

I dashed back to Garden Lodge ahead of Joe and Freddie. When they arrived I said nothing. This needed a plan. I decided not to try curtailing Freddie's activities, but to have some fun of my own. I asked Freddie if he'd mind if I went for a drink to my old haunt, the Market Tavern. He said it was fine and arranged for Terry Giddings, his new chauffeur, to drive me over there.

At the Tavern I had a few beers and got talking to a few old friends. They all said the same – I looked miserable.

'Here, pop this into your mouth,' said one, passing me something.

'What is it?' I asked.

'Doesn't matter what it is,' came the reply. 'Just pop it into your mouth. It'll cheer you up.' I could do with being cheered up, so without thinking I swallowed the pill. It was a tab of acid. Soon I was quite disorientated. The next thing I knew I'd left the Tavern with my friends and we were in Heaven.

No matter how much I had to drink, I never lost control of myself. But with acid I completely lost my bearings and turned into a zombie. At Heaven I met an old friend, Jay, whom I hadn't seen for years.

'What's the matter, Jim?' he asked. 'You look strange.'

I told him what I could remember, about starting at the Tavern, having swallowed something and now being on another planet. Fortunately, Jay took me under his wing for the rest of the night and made sure I came to no harm.

'You're not going back to your home tonight,' he told me. 'You'll stay at my place where you can be looked after.'

The next morning, waking up in Jay's flat, I had a humdinger of a headache. I assumed that back at Garden Lodge Freddie would be furious with me, so I set off for Mary's flat, where I figured I could explain what a ghastly time I'd had and why I'd stayed out all night. Mary told me that the previous night Freddie had been on the warpath for hours and stayed up all night, talking with Peter Straker, as he waited for me to come home.

Then the phone rang. It was Freddie.

'Jim's here,' she told him.

'Well,' he said, 'tell him to get back here, pack his bags and get out. He's to be gone by the time I get back from the studio.' Then he rang off.

I was homeless again. I left Mary's flat and stopped at a payphone to ring John Rowell to ask whether I could stay in his spare room again. He said I could, for as long as I wanted.

I returned to Garden Lodge, went to the bedroom and packed all my things. Then I went to John's flat. I came to the conclusion that Freddie and I had fallen out for good. A few days later, on the day *Time* opened, I got home and the phone was ringing. It was Freddie.

'Are you coming home?' he asked.

'No,' I said.

'But I want you to come to the opening night of *Time* with me,' he said softly.

'Well, you can take your friend with you. The dinner suit will fit him just as well,' I said.

'Come over,' he insisted. 'Let's chat about it.'

So I took a cab over and was met by Joe.

'He's upstairs waiting for you,' he said. As I stepped into the bedroom Freddie threw his arms around me. Without saying a word we fell into bed and made love. The first thing Freddie said afterwards was: 'Come on back home.' So I agreed. Then we got ready to go to *Time*. Freddie made it very plain it was only me he wanted by his side at the theatre that night, and after that things settled back into a happy routine.

During the interval at the show Freddie decided he wanted to sell ice creams. But things soon got out of hand and he started lobbing the ices randomly at members of the audience. Freddie was in equally high spirits at the after-show party held at the Hippodrome in Leicester Square where he introduced me to Cliff Richard as 'My man Jim'. Cliff's longevity in the music business was something Freddie told me he admired. Even though at the time he'd been in the business seventeen years himself, he still felt like a newcomer next to Cliff.

When Freddie told Dave Clark how much he admired Laurence Olivier, Dave arranged a private supper with Olivier and his wife Joan Plowright. Freddie told me that over supper the conversation got around to the critics and Freddie moaned about the scathing attacks he often suffered in the press. Olivier's response had been sublime.

'Fuck the critics!' he said.

When Freddie got home that night he was more star-struck than I had ever seen him.

'I've met one of the greats,' he said, beaming like an excited child.

Another day I got home and Freddie told me he'd had the unlikeliest of visitors who had turned up at Garden Lodge for the unlikeliest of reasons. It was Dustin Hoffman, looking for interior design ideas for one of his own homes.

The American actor wanted to commission an interior designer whom Freddie had used to carry out some of his ideas at Garden Lodge. He rang to ask Freddie if he could show Dustin some of the rooms he had worked on in the house, and Freddie was delighted. For an hour or so Garden Lodge became a show-house to beat all show-houses.

Freddie said Dustin was much shorter than he'd expected, terribly polite and rather nervous. But Freddie soon put him at his ease and gave him a tour of his handiwork and they talked about interior design, theatre and rock music. Freddie said he'd been in seventh heaven.

During the first half of the year Freddie, Brian, Roger and John were in the studio again in London and Munich, putting the final touches to their album *A Kind of Magic*. They would start around noon and work through for the next twelve hours. Freddie would get home from work at the earliest some time after ten, but rarely later than one in the morning. He'd bounce in and play me a demo tape of his latest song, giving a running commentary about the bits he felt still needed honing or new effects yet to be added. Best of all, some days he came in and played his tape without saying a word – it was finished and he knew it was good.

The single 'A Kind of Magic' came out in March and the video to accompany it was made at the then dilapidated Playhouse Theatre in Northumberland Avenue. I turned up after work one day to watch Freddie and take a look at how the video was getting on. Before long we almost came to blows when Freddie showed his jealous side.

I got used to hanging around on the sets of the video shoots, and that evening sat alone somewhere towards the back of the stalls to watch Freddie. One of the band's drivers came over and we got chatting; eventually we went off to have a drink. When I got back to the theatre Freddie was in his caravan, parked in the street near the stage door.

He looked very angry and I knew it was best not to hang around, so I kept out of his sight until it was time to go home. In the car on the way back to Garden Lodge Freddie turned to me and said: 'I'm disgusted with you. Who told you to bring your boyfriend in to see the video?'

I looked at him and burst out laughing.

'That wasn't a friend of mine,' I said, 'It was one of your band's bloody chauffeurs!'

Freddie could also show his sense of humour. In 1986 I got a St Patrick's Day card from Freddie. That evening I was told I wasn't allowed into the kitchen. Joe or Phoebe passed a cup of coffee out to me to keep me quiet. Then Joe told me dinner was ready. I made for the kitchen, but my way was barred.

'You're in the dining room,' he said. 'Freddie's given me strict instructions to make a special dinner for you because it's St Patrick's Day.'

In the dining room the table was fully laid for one, complete with lit candelabra. And on a plate was a large juicy steak surrounded by small bowls – spuds prepared in every conceivable way: roast, sautéed, mashed, boiled, croquette, chips, *Dauphinoise*, baked, and so on.

'Freddie told us to cook every type of potato we could think of,' Joe said. Freddie always thought that because I was Irish I had to love potatoes. I did. I sat down and ate the most delicious dinner I can remember.

A few times during the year Freddie took me out for romantic suppers. One night I got home from work and he hugged me as usual.

'Go and get yourself ready. We're going out,' he said.

Terry drove us to one of Freddie's favourite places to eat, an Indian restaurant called Shazan's. But we went alone and, unusually, there were none of Freddie's friends waiting for him. He'd requested the most romantic table in the restaurant, which was in the basement.

All through dinner he kept touching me, perhaps to see if he could embarrass me in front of the other customers. He'd reach across the table and hold my hand. When the ice cream arrived he even spoon-fed me mouthfuls. His attitude to the looks of disdain from some of the people there was 'Fuck them!' But it wasn't mine. Though he was trying to be romantic, in front of all those strangers I felt very shy and turned bright scarlet.

When Freddie and I were in private he could be particularly

romantic. We never once broached the subject of how long we'd be together. We just accepted that we were and would be. Occasionally he'd ask me what I wanted out of life.

'Contentment and to be loved,' I'd reply. It seemed like I'd found both in Freddie.

Another thing he'd often tell me, right up until the night he died, was: 'I love you.' And it was never an 'I love you' which just rolled off the tongue; he always meant it.

I didn't find it so easy to show emotion. I'd lived on the London gay scene for many years and had come to realise you can get hurt very easily when relationships end. Each finished relationship builds up a new barrier and they become difficult to break down. But, in time, Freddie tore them all down.

I think we both shared a fear of the same thing – loneliness. You can have all the friends in the world around you, yet still feel agonisingly lonely, as Freddie said time and again. We were both acutely aware that many of our gay friends were haunted by the prospect of living out their lives alone, unwanted and unloved.

Freddie's next solo release was 'Time' in May. The same month Queen headlined the annual Golden Rose rock festival in Montreux. I went with Freddie on the trip and the concert was followed by a party for the band on a boat.

When Freddie arrived he was asked to pose for the photographers, and I soon realised that he actually did have some power over the press. The photo session went very well and after five or ten minutes, when they'd got plenty of pictures, Freddie thanked them, said he'd finished and it was time for the celebrations to start.

He sat down at a table and started chatting intently to singer Belouis Some, who was always changing his name and seeking Freddie's advice on the subject. A few minutes later a sneaky freelance photographer crept up on them to try for more candid shots of Freddie. But he'd barely fired off three shots before five of the other photographers pounced on him. They dragged him away and a bit of a scuffle followed.

'I bet you won't see that photo in the press tomorrow,'

shrieked Freddie gleefully. He was right. It's also just as well that no photographs were taken during the party; what happened on the boat that night doesn't bear thinking about. It was a riot.

The *Sun* did later print a photograph of Freddie taken while he was performing at the festival, which he didn't appreciate. It showed off "Flabulous Freddie" with a slight paunch, wickedly describing it as his "midriff bulge". When he saw the picture he looked at me and shook his head in despair.

'It's typical,' he said. 'If I'm slim the papers say I'm too thin and if I put on a little bit of a belly they say I'm too fat. It's a no-win situation.'

Freddie joined the band to rehearse for their forthcoming 'Magic' Tour of Europe. It was to begin at the Rasunda Fotboll Stadion in Stockholm on 7 June, then continue until August, finishing with the most fantastic of flourishes before Queen's biggest-ever British audience of 120,000 at Knebworth Park, Hertfordshire.

As they left Britain in June, the album *A Kind of Magic* was released, along with the single 'Friends Will Be Friends'; 'Seven Seas of Rye', Queen's second single from 1974, which had given them their first taste of chart success, was on the B-side. The album rose to the top of the charts in Britain and over thirty other countries.

When the Magic Tour reached Paris I decided to make a surprise visit to see Freddie. It was a gamble. Although Freddie loved springing surprises on others, he hated being caught off-guard himself.

After work I went home and changed, filled a holdall and set out for Heathrow. I flew to Paris and made my way to the Royal Monceau Hotel. I asked if they had anyone staying in the name of Freddie Mercury or Queen and the receptionists just gave me a blank look. I knew I had the right hotel and guessed that the band were checked in under aliases to avoid the press and fans. (I later discovered that Freddie always booked under the name A. Mason.)

Happily, I bumped into one of the crew in the lobby and he confirmed that Freddie was indeed staying there. He and the band had gone to the Hippodrome de Vincennes for a sound-check. So I sat and waited. When Freddie returned he looked at me and said casually: 'Oh, hello.'

He didn't seem surprised to see me; if anything he looked angry. Later he had a go at Joe for not telling him I was arriving; he did need to be in control of events.

The next morning Diana Moseley arrived at our hotel suite. She was the costume designer for the Magic Tour and was delivering for the first time Freddie's campest costume, a deep red cloak trimmed in fake ermine and a jewelled crown fit for royalty. It was extraordinary to watch him as he threw the cloak over his white towelling robe, put on his crown and strutted around the room.

Freddie sashayed around regally but said something was missing. Then he grabbed a banana and used it as a microphone. He flounced about, trying to work out the way the cloak fell as he moved. He loved it. And so did all the fans that night.

As the crowds cheered, I thought: 'That's my man!'

The following Saturday, 21 June, Queen played the Maimaritgelände, in Mannheim, Germany. At about four on the Sunday morning I was at Garden Lodge when the phone rang. It was Freddie, screaming that he'd been locked in his room and couldn't get out. He was depressed and wanted me to fly out immediately to be with him. When I got to the hotel Freddie seemed fine, if slightly exhausted. It was nice to feel wanted.

After Berlin we went on to Munich. No sooner had we arrived at the hotel than Freddie flounced out. He'd been given a very plain, drab suite and it was not to his liking. We settled into our hotel rooms, then joined the rest of the band for dinner in a tiny café. We had a raucous meal and all got terribly drunk. I remember talking a lot to Roger Taylor's roadie, Chris 'Crystal' Taylor, and Brian's assistant

Jobby. The party continued through most of the night back at the hotel.

From Munich the band went on to Zurich, but I headed back to London. On 5 July they played Dublin, where they had the only poor reception of the tour. Several drunken gate-crashers got in and started throwing things at Freddie and the others. After that night Freddie vowed that the band would never return to Ireland again. Nor did they.

Finally the band played Newcastle before returning to London for a few very special days.

Friday, 11 July and Saturday, 12 July were milestones in Queen's career – two sell-out concerts at Wembley Stadium. It was the band's first time back on the massive stage since their incredible show-stealing *Live Aid* set a year earlier, and over the two nights 150,000 people would see them.

Freddie had recurring problems with nodules on his vocal cords, the price he paid for being a singer. That meant he toured with a small machine, a steam inhaler in which he firmly believed. He also sucked Strepsils throat lozenges all the time. On the first night of Wembley Freddie had some throat problems, but dismissed them as not drastic enough to stop the show. As always, I watched from all over Wembley on both nights.

The after-show party on Saturday was held at the Roof Gardens Club in Kensington and, because the press would be there, Freddie wanted Mary on his arm. It was a rare deceit that he was not in love with me, and he apologised for it.

'It's got to be this way because of the press,' he said.

I understood completely, and followed at a safe distance a few paces behind them.

The party was a characteristically lavish Queen affair. Hundred of bottles of champagne were emptied, and the final bill was over £80,000.

The five hundred or so guests were greeted in the lifts by girls dressed in nothing more than body paintings by German artist Bernd Bauer. Plenty of famous names turned up: Jeff Beck, Nick Rhodes from Duran Duran, Spandau Ballet, Paul

King, Limahl, Cliff Richard, Gary Glitter, Mel Smith, Griff Rhys Jones, Janet Street Porter and Fish from Marillion, someone I really took to.

At one point Queen took to the stage to belt out rock and roll numbers and Freddie stole the show with an unlikely partner, Page Three model Samantha Fox. He hauled Sam on to the stage and they tore into 'Tutti Frutti' and 'Sweet Little Rock and Roller'. When I met her afterwards she was still shaking with excitement.

Next stop on the Magic Tour was Manchester's Maine Road football stadium on Wednesday, 16 July, and I flew up north with Freddie and the band. For the show Mary, Phoebe and I wanted to sit in the audience. A steward escorted us to three seats. About ten minutes later three people turned up and claimed the seats were theirs. Mary flew into a rage and tried pulling rank, telling them she was Freddie Mercury's girlfriend. It wasn't a clever move; her remark didn't cut any ice. In fact, she found herself at the receiving end of an unpleasant tirade from an obnoxious man. (I was later told he was Peter Moores, heir to the Littlewood's Pools empire.) In the end we gave up the seats and watched the rest of the show from backstage.

After the concert we were escorted through the cheering crowds of fans. At one point there was a serious risk that the band would be mobbed, so we resorted to a double-decker bus with a difference – instead of ordinary doors you got in through a custom-built 'tunnel'. To make a quick getaway, Mary and I and some others from the team were waiting on the coach ahead of the band. When they ran on we all hurried upstairs to see the sea of cheering faces stretching back in every direction. What a send-off!

We pulled off with a police escort, sirens blazing and the night sky lit up with flashing blue lights. We had a clear run out of the city and our escort went on for miles past the city boundary. During that journey back to London I pondered the scenes I'd just witnessed. They reminded me of the newsreel footage of the Beatles being mobbed by fans in the sixties. For the first time I fully appreciated how frightening it could sometimes be for Queen, and why they needed such elaborate security arrangements to escape a mob of tens of thousands of thrilled but over-excited fans.

After the Manchester concert Freddie left with Joe for the next leg of the tour – Cologne and Vienna. Queen were playing Budapest on Sunday, 27 July, making history as the first major Western rock band to perform in an open-air stadium behind the Iron Curtain. The band decided to take a river cruise down the Danube for a few days before arriving in Budapest in great style on President Gorbachev's personal hydrofoil.

Mary rarely accompanied Freddie on tours, but on this trip he wanted to give her a short holiday, so he invited her to Vienna to join him for the cruise. Mary was very worried about leaving Jerry, the cat she'd inherited from Freddie, so I volunteered to stay in her flat for a few days to keep an eye on him.

But I wasn't planning on missing 'The Hungarian Experience', as it had been dubbed. The Queen office in London arranged for me to fly to Budapest a few days early, on the Friday. Terry and Joe were waiting for me at the airport with a chauffeur-driven car; we went directly to the hotel, where Freddie had claimed the Presidential Suite. It was magnificent, with a vast balcony, and was crowded with people including Mary, Freddie and Queen's manager Jim Beach, Brian May, John Deacon, Roger Taylor, who was having his neck muscles worked on by the band's physiotherapist, and paparazzo Richard Young.

After making a sound-check we all headed out for a huge Hungarian feast, with every damn thing tasting of paprika. When we returned to the hotel, I sloped off for a quiet stroll around the streets of this enchanting city before finally turning in for the night.

It was difficult enough in Hungary to buy records and cassettes, so heaven knows how impossible it would have been to buy any of the eighty thousand tickets for the concert.

For most of the inhabitants of Budapest, the tickets were too expensive – they cost the equivalent of a month's wages.

As a special treat for his audience, Freddie decided to thank Queen's dedicated followers by singing 'Tavaszi Szel', a moving and traditional Hungarian song. He was only given the lyrics late on the afternoon of the show, so he spent all his time striding around the suite or balcony frantically trying to teach himself the words. They didn't come very easily.

Queen's presence in Budapest had set the place buzzing, and when we left for the stadium our police escort brought the city to a complete standstill. We made the twenty-minute journey at breakneck speed in the first of a fleet of limousines flanked by scores of police outriders. We screeched around corners, jumped lights and seemed to fly through the city. Terry, Joe and I were nervous about the speed, but Freddie was quite oblivious to being tossed around so roughly. He was still trying to remember the words of the Hungarian song, humming to himself and repeating the lyrics beneath his breath.

The concert that night was sensational. There were police everywhere at the Nepstadion to control the massive crowd. I watched the first half of the set from the wings; but after the interval I went out front and spent the rest of the evening lost among the ecstatic crowd. I watched my man, spellbound, from all points in the stadium. The stage was massive and Freddie used it all, exhaustively working the audience. Above the stage were vast torches belching flames, and the whole thing looked spectacular.

When Freddie came to sing the folk song, he was astounding. He had scribbled the lyrics on his hand and resorted to them openly, but it didn't matter. As soon as the first words sprang from his mouth, the whole audience of Hungarians went wild, stunned that a foreigner had braved their most famous and difficult song. At the end the crowd erupted and, even though he was no more than a dot on the horizon, I could tell that Freddie was relieved to have got through it. Towards the end of the concert, Freddie strode out in his ermine cape and crown and the stadium exploded into total euphoria. For hours after that show Freddie was on an unstoppable high.

Next morning Joe had a slight drama. He wore contact lenses but had forgotten to bring their small cases on tour, so instead he placed them to soak in two glasses of water. He was not in his room when the chambermaid called and she emptied the glasses into the sink, flushing his lenses away.

'Hopeless fool!' said Freddie. I wasn't sure if he was referring to the chambermaid or Joe.

When I got back to Britain I read a feature by David Wigg in the *Daily Express*. He reported Freddie's response to Mary's desire to have a baby by him: he would sooner have another cat. David also reported that Freddie was unattached. Freddie always felt that keeping to this line made things simpler for the two of us, and he was right. However, he did say in the article: 'For the first time I've found a contentment within myself.' He told me he was referring to our relationship.

Freddie felt Mary had long since become a public part of his life in the papers and knew she could deal with it easily enough. But he always tried to shield me from the press. He looked on fame as a double-edged sword.

After work on Friday, 1 August I flew to Barcelona to join Freddie. He told me he'd been interviewed by Spanish television and declared cheekily that the main reason he was in Spain was in the hope of meeting their great opera diva, Montserrat Caballé. Phoebe had converted Freddie to opera. He had a large collection of opera CDs and probably everything Montserrat Caballé had ever recorded. Freddie would spend hours listening to them and asking Phoebe to explain the characters, plots and sub-plots.

After the Barcelona concert we all went out to a fabulous fish restaurant. At one point I asked Roger Taylor how the tour was going.

'Well, Freddie's different this year,' he said. 'What have you done to him?'

He told me Freddie was a decidedly changed man. He'd stopped trawling the gay venues while the others went back to their hotel, and he'd stopped burning the candle at both ends.

Roger's comment spoke volumes. I took it as a reassuring nod of approval which was very much appreciated. Coming from one of Freddie's closest friends, and one of the band, I saw it as a vote of confidence in our affair. To me it said: 'There has to be something serious going on here, Jim.'

From the restaurant we went on to a stylish nightclub co-owned by a stunning-looking woman in a rather revealing dress. She decided she wanted to join our party and made a bee-line for Freddie, forcing herself between Freddie and me. Her right buttock was precariously perched on half of his chair and her left on half of mine. She then crossed her legs and, every so often, her hand slipped to her side as she yanked her hemline a little higher up her tanned legs.

'Have you got a girlfriend?' she asked Freddie.

'No, I haven't,' he replied.

'Have you got a wife?' she asked.

He leaned across her, put his hand on my knee and said: 'Yes. This is the wife!'

With that the poor woman almost died! She babbled hurried excuses and ran off into the crowd to hide.

The next date of the tour was a Sunday night in Madrid. Before we left Barcelona I arranged for some flowers to be delivered to Freddie's hotel room in Madrid ahead of our arrival. The message on them was to read: 'From the wife!'

When we got to Madrid there was no sign of the flowers anywhere. They turned up several hours later and looked to be in a sorry state: a scruffy little bunch of half-dead roses. Worse still, the message said something about a 'Whiff'. Freddie spent most of the day trying to fathom out what 'Whiff' meant, so in the end I put him out of his misery and told him of my intentions which had gone wrong. He burst out laughing.

Back in Britain, Queen were due to play Knebworth Park, in Stevenage, Hertfordshire, on Saturday, 9 August. It was the last concert Queen ever played. That was a corker of a day and the whole event was a great way for any rock legend to bow out from live performances. I flew up with Freddie, Brian, Roger and John in a helicopter from the helipad in Battersea. There were said to be 120,000 at Knebworth that day, and some sources reckoned it was as many as 200,000. The traffic jams brought the whole of the surrounding countryside to a halt. Still some miles from Knebworth, I looked out of the helicopter window on to the endless ribbons of tiny cars, sitting bumper to bumper.

'Are we causing all this?' Freddie asked.

'Yes,' I replied.

'Oh,' he said softly, grinning.

When the helicopter landed, cars were standing by to ferry the band directly to their dressing rooms. I followed in another car and met Freddie in his room. He was always nervous before a show. In the minutes before it was time to go on he seemed to have too much nervous energy in him and would become terribly on edge. This restlessness lasted right up until the very second he hit the ramp to the stage; but once he'd seen the heads of the fans, he was fine. He was theirs.

At the other concerts I'd often go into the audience and head for the sound tower to clamber up for a perfect view. At Knebworth I couldn't even get to the tower through the dense crowd. I milled around on the edge for most of the night. Towards the end of the concert, a familiar face approached me. It belonged to a guy I'd met in Budapest who told me he'd been granted special permission to fly from Hungary to attend the Queen night at Knebworth. I was so touched that I took him backstage to meet Freddie, and the Hungarian was overjoyed.

As always, the concert was followed by a legendary Queen party, though Freddie and the band couldn't stay all night because the helicopter was standing by to fly us back to London. During that flight we heard a rumour that a fan had died, the victim of a stabbing. Because of the sheer numbers of fans it had not been possible to get him to an ambulance in time to save his life. When Freddie heard about this he was very upset.

The next morning Joe confirmed Freddie's worst fears; it was now official. A fan *had* died after a knife attack. Freddie seemed very subdued but appeared to cheer up once friends arrived for Sunday lunch. When I went out for the Sunday papers I was expecting the worst from the tabloids, dreading what they would have to say about Queen's farewell concert. To my amazement I couldn't find a single bad word about them, despite the fan's tragic death. The good coverage in the press cheered Freddie up a little, but the death continued to prey on his mind. He only ever wanted his music to bring happiness.

While the rest of us took the remainder of the day very slowly, Freddie had his mind on the future. Even though he'd just notched up his biggest-ever triumph in Britain, he immediately had his mind on his next project. He wanted to get back into the studio.

First, though, over the next few weeks Freddie planned to relax and do some serious socialising. He wanted to throw a fortieth birthday party for himself at Garden Lodge. Then he and I, accompanied by Joe, would go off to Japan for what Freddie promised me would be 'the holiday of a lifetime'.

Freddie spent a great deal of time planning his birthday. He decided on a Mad Hat party and sent out over two hundred invitations for the afternoon of Sunday, 7 September. Some guests were so keen that two of Freddie's friends from the Royal Ballet turned up a week early, complete with outrageous headgear.

I wanted to give Freddie something very special for a very special birthday: a gold wedding ring. It was to be a secret, so to discover his ring size I tried on an old battered one which Winnie had given him but was now relegated to the bottom of a bedroom drawer. It fitted my little finger perfectly, and on that basis I went off and bought Freddie a plain, flat gold band. I mentioned I was buying it to Mary, who thought it a lovely idea.

During the week leading up to the party the weather was consistently overcast. Freddie wanted his guests to have the full run of the house and garden, so we prayed hard for good weather and even considered sun-dancing. The days immediately before the party were largely spent stocking up with provisions and decking Garden Lodge from top to toe with flowers. Freddie was so meticulous that he personally oversaw every detail. Joe, Phoebe and I simply did our master's bidding.

The garden was something of a mess, because Freddie was having a pool so that he could keep Japanese koi fish. There was still a huge hole in the middle of the garden and Freddie was concerned about guests falling in and seriously hurting themselves.

On Thursday, the night before Freddie's birthday, several people were at the house. Peter Straker was there, which meant he and Freddie would be up all night. Just before I went to bed, I called Freddie into the dining room. 'I wanted you to have this first thing in the morning when you got up,' I said, passing him the box with the ring in it. He opened it up and tried on the ring at once. It fitted a treat. Then he kissed me and we cuddled for a minute or two.

He was never a jewellery queen, wearing little chains and twee bracelets. But he always wore the ring around the house. However, if he went out in public he'd usually slip it off. Gay or straight, a ring on your wedding finger tells the world that you're attached. He wanted to give nothing away.

On the Saturday I was out shopping and came up with the answer to the problem of the garden hole. I bought hundreds of barbecue candles and night lights to mark out the dangerous area.

When we woke up on Sunday morning the clear blue skies promised sunshine all day. In the morning, as I placed my candles around the edge of the pit in the garden, Freddie was looking out from the window, confounded and bemused. When I came in he asked me what I'd been doing. I wanted the candles to be a surprise, so I said, 'You'll see this evening.'

The party got going by early afternoon amid colourful scenes to rival any Easter bonnet parade. Every guest turned out in a hat, ranging from the conservative to the crazy. Diana Moseley had laid on several hats for Freddie, made by different designers, but in the end he settled mostly for just one, a 'bongo' hat sending up the fad of wobbly things bouncing around on the end of two wires. I wore a big floppy hat, made from foam and covered with flower ribbons pinched from the birthday bouquets which had been arriving all week for Freddie.

Joe's hat was good enough to eat – a box of chocolates with real chocolates on top. And Phoebe sported one which was a tribute to Miss Piggy. Mary wore a matador's hat speared with a sword. All the band were there with their respective partners. I remember Jim Beach, Peter Straker, Trevor Clarke, Dave Clark, Tim Rice, Elaine Paige and Susannah York all having a good time. (Wayne Sleep was also there, but it was a doomed friendship; Freddie complained that once he had had a drink too many he became 'a right pain' and left him off the guest list for future parties.)

I, too, had a few friends there, including John Rowell who came in a hat boasting a tiny laid-up table complete with miniature cups and saucers.

The party lasted well into the early hours but, as I had to go to work the next day, I slipped up to the bedroom and got into bed. Just as I was dozing off, I heard the door open. It was Freddie showing friends around the house. 'Sshh,' he whispered, 'my husband's asleep. Don't wake him.' A little later I heard loud screams of laughter from downstairs and knew that Freddie and Straker were in party mood. I drifted off, never believing that I would be able to sleep through the din.

When I woke up, in bed alone, I could hear voices coming from downstairs. Freddie and Straker had talked through the night and were still in a strange mood. I got up and dressed for work in my suit with a white shirt and a tie. I popped in to say hello and goodbye to them, then went into the hall to put on my overcoat. As I crossed the double door to the lounge, I overheard Freddie asking Peter Straker: 'Who was that?'

'It's your husband, darling.'

Freddie screamed.

I still don't think Freddie had recognised me in a suit. Even though he'd bought me two suits for my birthday, he never paid much attention to what I was wearing.

When I got home from work that night he said as much. He told me that that was the first time he'd noticed me in a suit. I took it as his way of telling me he thought I looked smart.

4

A YEN TO SHOP

A few days after Freddie's Mad Hat party, Queen bounced back into the charts with 'Who Wants to Live Forever'. This kept Freddie feeling on top of the world as we took off for our Japanese holiday at the end of September 1986. It was a trip of a lifetime, and cost Freddie well over £1 million. Joe packed Freddie's cases – one for shirts and socks, another for jeans and jackets.

Freddie had been to Japan before and liked to regale me with stories of his previous visits. 'Really, the best time to go out is the spring when the azaleas are in bloom,' he said. Azaleas were his favourite. He also said he was looking forward to buying things in Japan for Garden Lodge. He had finally set his heart on transforming the house, which still had bare walls and empty rooms, into a proper home for us all.

Our hostess during our Japanese trip was Misa Watanabe, who handled all Queen's affairs in Japan. Freddie bought her an exquisite Lalique lead crystal vase as a present. It was made in France but prohibitively expensive to buy in Japan. The vase was far too delicate to be entrusted to baggage handlers, so we took it with us as hand luggage. But when we went through security, to Freddie's annoyance the vase failed to show up on the X-ray machine and the security people demanded we open it.

We flew out first-class on a direct twelve-hour Japan

57

Airlines flight to Tokyo. When we touched down at about four in the afternoon local time Misa Watanabe, a slight, stylish woman in her forties, was waiting to greet us. She'd also arranged for a small contingent of hysterical Freddie fans to be there, too.

Freddie introduced me with: 'This is Jim, my new man.' Then he whispered to her quietly for a minute. Although I couldn't hear what they were saying, I could tell it was about me – and I didn't need a university degree to realise his words were complimentary. Also waiting at the airport for Freddie was another trusted friend of his, Itami, a former bodyguard who owned a private security company and always looked after Freddie in Japan.

The drive into Tokyo took a good hour, weaving slowly through bumper-to-bumper rush-hour traffic. And when the car stopped it wasn't at the hotel but outside a massive department store called Seibu. The shop had stayed open specially for Freddie, the ultimate shopper. He was in his element as he was greeted by an endless line of meticulously attentive managers and sales assistants.

Freddie shopped for the next four hours. There were at least seven floors, and we combed each one for beautiful things to buy. Freddie's battle cry was 'Shop till you drop.' He bought a lacquered cabinet in purple, cups, bowls, chopstick-rests and dozens of pairs of chopsticks – some, costing £75 each, rippled with real gold and silver strands. Everything was ridiculously expensive.

Freddie was already getting ten per cent discount, but Misa ran around behind Freddie demanding that the assistants put everything on her account. 'If it's charged to me I'll get a further fifteen per cent off,' she trilled. So Freddie was really on twenty-five per cent discount.

Freddie could have gone on shopping all night. He loved everything Japanese so much he seemed to want to own everything in sight. Eventually he was dragged away. Standing outside on the pavement, I was fascinated by the teeming streets filled with little black heads darting about quickly and smoothly like large worker ants. The speedy, noisy activity at pedestrian crossings was another remarkable sight: just a buzzing blur.

I drank in everything and Freddie smiled. 'If a natural blonde walked by, immaterial of sex, everyone would stop and stare,' he observed. At last we drove to our hotel.

We were staying at the Ocura. When we arrived, we discovered that Misa had reserved Freddie the hotel's extraordinary Emperor's Suite – a penthouse like no other. It was so large it even boasted a smaller self-contained suite for private staff to stay in. The main doors led into a long hallway, and through a door on the right was a magnificent L-shaped sitting room walled in glass looking out over mesmerising views of the city. The master bedroom had a massive en suite bathroom with a sunken bath big enough for ten. Joe's rooms, the suite within, included his own kitchen and sitting room.

Misa had arranged for chilled champagne and canapés to be waiting. Freddie gave Misa the now only partly wrapped Lalique vase, apologising profusely for its sorry-looking state. It made no difference; Misa was delighted. Then trays of Japanese food started arriving and everyone tucked in. When Misa and her team finally left, Freddie and I turned in.

He soon drifted off to sleep, but not me. I had my first taste of jet-lag and it drove me to distraction. At four in the morning I couldn't lie awake any longer, so to relieve the monotony I got up and started watching Japanese television, with the volume barely audible so as not to wake his nibs. I didn't go back to bed that night; I just waited for Freddie to wake up.

We had breakfast in the middle of the morning, and by noon we were ready to 'shop! shop! shop!' all over again. Itami was waiting outside the suite as we emerged, and accompanied us to the lobby. Here four or five quiet fans were waiting patiently for Freddie, each bearing a small, exquisitely wrapped gift. As Freddie thanked them, signed autographs and posed for photographs, I was told that this particular group of Queen fans were so dedicated they followed the band everywhere they went around the world.

One of the first ports of call on the shopping trip was a very modern fashion designer called Jun, whose trendy clothes Freddie adored. From there we moved to a shop called Beverly Hills, where Freddie fell in love with a suit. It was a cross between tan and grey in colour and had a shiny finish, an effect Freddie loved. The trouble was, the suit was too big for him. Then Freddie looked around and found another suit he liked which did fit. So he turned to me and said, 'Why don't you try the other suit on?' I did, and it fitted perfectly. But I said I didn't want it and gave it back to the assistant.

We ran around buying shirts at Beverly Hills, then went to other boutiques nearby. In one Freddie spent more than two hours buying silk ties, including a number of white ones, most costing £75 or more. He picked out and bought several ties for me, even though I'd already bought some.

Until that day I don't think Freddie had ever owned a tie in his life. But he quickly made up for lost time in that shop, because he must have bought over a hundred. The silliest thing about the tie-shopping experience was that Freddie couldn't actually knot a tie. He was a magpie and loved buying things to hoard, knowing perfectly well that he'd be lucky to get around to wearing everything even once. Whenever he wanted to wear one he usually came looking for me. 'Jim!' he'd call out hopelessly, 'Help me, will you?' When it came to settling his bill he actually ran out of cash, having set out with wads of the stuff. Joe and I emptied our wallets and pooled what we had to make up the shortfall. If we hadn't come up with enough to bail Freddie out, he would simply have reserved all the ties and sent one of us over to pay for them later.

We went to the Ginza, an area of Tokyo similar to London's Soho and packed with electronic gadgetry shops. Freddie was not very good with electronic gadgets but marvelled at hi-tech wizardry. He spent another fortune on several personal organisers, and when we got outside he gave me one of them.

Back at the hotel we could barely get into the hallway. All the things Freddie had bought at Seibu had been delivered. The boxes were stacked high on either side and represented Freddie's £250,000 shopping spree.

It became clear that, large as the Emperor Suite was, it would be impractical to have all Freddie's shopping sent to the hotel. So from then on everything was sent directly to the warehouse for shipping home. It became Joe's job painstakingly to list all Freddie's purchases.

That evening Freddie, Joe and I went out to dinner with Misa and a friend to an elegant rooftop restaurant. Freddie wanted to wear a new shirt, but it was badly creased. I'm not sure why we didn't think to send down for an iron, but instead Joe tried to think of alternative ways to remove the creases.

I came up with the answer: a metal hot-plate which was keeping some snacks warm in our sitting room. I turned it upside down and, with a bit of fumbling, Joe and I managed to iron the shirt.

'Clever bitch, aren't you?' said Freddie.

'I have my uses!' I replied.

We each donned suits for the occasion, Freddie wearing the one he'd bought at Beverly Hills. It was the first time I'd ever seen him in a suit and tie, and I have to say he looked great.

Preferring to stick to Western food, Freddie, Joe and I tore into succulent steaks which in Japan cost an arm and a leg. After dinner we set out to visit a few gay clubs, including one which was a transvestite bar. As soon as we approached, the doorman recognised Misa and greeted her excitedly as 'Mama Misa'. We sat down at a table and enjoyed the non-stop drag cabaret.

At one point a girl approached Freddie and was told to move along, so she came and sat next to me instead, chatting away in clipped pidgin English. A second hostess arrived, there to encourage the customers to enjoy themselves and drink a lot. 'Go easy on the drinks,' Freddie whispered. 'They'll try to make you buy more.' Later, as we got up to leave, Freddie said: 'Did you know that those girls with us were both blokes?' I was speechless; I had had no idea.

In our first week in Tokyo Misa threw a birthday party for herself at her home. The three of us arrived, this time in dinner suits. Although Freddie drew the line at wearing a black tie, he looked sensational in a light blue silk waistcoat. On the way over we'd wondered whether, according to Japanese custom, we'd have to remove our shoes on entering her home. But while Misa was terribly Japanese, much of her house had a very Western feel to it. Our footwear remained firmly on our feet.

When it was time for the birthday cake, two arrived, the first decorated in plain white icing, for Misa, the other with a red, white and blue Union Jack on it, for Freddie.

'As I missed your birthday party,' she told Freddie, 'I thought I'd have this party for you as well.'

That night Freddie became deeply engrossed in conversation with a Japanese artist and talked about commissioning a painting from him. Freddie explained how he wanted the picture to look, even suggesting with his hand flourishes of the brushstrokes.

On another night Misa arranged a surprise outing. We only knew were going to see a show, not a special event, so the three of us dressed in lounge suits and left by car. The journey was madness. We trickled along at a snail's pace because of the traffic, and what would have taken little more than ten minutes by foot took forever by car. We turned up a good half-hour late. What Misa hadn't told Freddie – and as it caught him totally off guard he was not pleased – was that he was guest of honour at the glittering *opening* night of Andrew Lloyd Webber's musical *Cats*. Everything had been held up just for him.

Misa rushed the three of us into the hospitality room, where Freddie was introduced to the other VIPs. Then his arrival was announced in the vast auditorium, a massive marquee. As he and Misa were escorted to their front row seats, the entire house got to its feet to give him a standing ovation. Joe and I, meanwhile, were escorted to two seats at the back of the stalls.

Cats was staged entirely in Japanese and had been reworked from the original London production. Although I did not know a word of Japanese, the performance was thoroughly absorbing. As a special favour, Misa asked Freddie to call on one of the principal actors backstage after the show. He agreed on condition that he wouldn't have to meet all the rest of the company. He was on holiday, and that seemed like too much hard work.

But after we met the star in her dressing room Freddie, to his horror, was taken to meet the *entire* cast. Worse still, they were in party mood. There was no means of escape without being rude, so we ended up staying several hours. Later that evening, back at the hotel, Freddie showed his anger at Misa for not warning him he would have to be the guest of honour, that it was a black-tie evening and that he would have to meet the cast.

But then Misa arranged an outing for Freddie that was so special it more than made up for the chaos of the *Cats* evening. He was taken to see the wonderful gardens and grounds of the Golden Palace, built by an early Emperor of Japan in the ancient city of Kyoto. We were due to make the journey by Japan's celebrated Bullet Train and were told to meet Misa at the station mid-morning. We were met by several of Misa's entourage, but no Misa.

The train left the platform and quickly accelerated – it got its name for a top speed of about 150mph. Freddie was convinced that Misa had missed the train.

'It wouldn't surprise me if she hired a helicopter and is waiting for us in Kyoto,' he said. Then a few minutes later she found us in our carriage.

Old Kyoto was astoundingly beautiful and filled with tiny antique shops which made it paradise for Freddie. Before we'd even got to the Golden Palace, Freddie insisted on doing some shopping. He bought an ornate *hibachi*, a sort of ancient portable terracotta barbecue, although it was not in the particular shade of blue Freddie wanted. And he bought four very tall antique candlesticks, lacquered in black and gold. They were four feet high and reminded me of the sort of things placed around coffins when lying in rest. Very morbid.

Although the Golden Palace was undergoing renovation work and closed to all visitors, Misa had arranged for Freddie to visit the many acres of perfectly manicured gardens. We walked around the grounds for several hours, inspecting every flower and shrub. Sadly Freddie's favourite, the azaleas, were not in bloom. But he was fascinated by the topiary, marvelling at the intricate shaping of the trees. Another favourite of his was a koi pool, where he was mesmerised by the prize golden carp.

Freddie delighted in running around as a tourist, snapping photographs of everything in sight. But he wasn't very practical with a camera. In fact he had no idea what he was doing and was hilarious to watch. When we got his first few rolls of film developed, the pictures were wildly out of focus. But he gradually seemed to learn from his mistakes and, after being told many times exactly what he was doing wrong, he got the hang of it. Then we couldn't stop him taking photographs by the dozen.

We left the grounds of the Golden Palace for our hotel just outside Kyoto. It was a daunting concrete monster on the Western model, vast and impersonal. But Freddie noticed that at the back of the hotel the tiered, landscaped garden was dotted with chalets, each boasting a futon and a bathroom but little else. They were traditional Japanese rooms.

'We're in Japan, so we must go Japanese,' decided Freddie, and we were given a room. First, though, Freddie decided to have afternoon tea. Just as I found somewhere to sit, he stopped me and motioned that we should move on. 'No,' he said. 'We're not going to sit there, we're going around the corner.'

I could hear the sound of lapping water, and when we turned the corner we found a stream running through the hotel, filled with koi. Even more surprising, behind thick plate-glass windows was a waterfall cascading into a pool. So against this backdrop we sat and had our tea. Freddie was buzzing with admiration for the hotel's wacky creativity and delighted in pointing it all out to me.

After tea we were shown through the garden to our traditional Japanese chalet. It was the furthest from the hotel, tucked right into the corner of the grounds. Inside there was one room with a futon and a small bathroom. In the latter there was nothing more sophisticated than a wooden tub, which we decided to try out at once. We undressed and I ran the bath, and when it was full I was just about to get in when Freddie squealed.

'No,' he said. 'You don't do that, that's not the way the Japanese do it. We're in Japan, we're going to have a Japanese bath.' Following his instructions I washed outside the tub, soaping myself and rinsing off using a little wooden cup. Only when you're clean do you get into the tub, simply to soak. Freddie also washed and rinsed and we got in to soak together. Freddie could always stay in the bath much longer than me; he was a real water baby.

The next thing Misa had lined up for us in Kyoto was a visit to a school for geisha girls. There we learned that they are part of a deep-seated tradition in Japan; to be a geisha is a proper profession, demanding about seven years of training. Freddie was engrossed, wanting to know everything. The girls' make-up fascinated him. He asked how the effects were created and how long the whole process took. And Freddie adored the colourful kimonos they were wearing, made of fine silks and designed with large square sleeves.

We were introduced to the teacher, or *madam*, a little old lady who had one tooth in her wizened head and played a one-stringed banjo, singing along as the girls danced around for our entertainment and delight. We sat cross-legged at their feet and took part in a traditional tea ceremony.

Afterwards we headed off to a fashionable nightclub where Freddie was, of course, the centre of attention. Everyone seemed to want to meet him. The one person Freddie took a shine to was a witty drag queen in 'civvies' introduced to us by Misa. Freddie nicknamed him HeShe, and when the bar later closed HeShe invited us back to his home for drinks. At HeShe's everyone gossiped and giggled and had a great time, but I was so shattered by jet-lag that I stretched out on the floor and dozed off, Japanese-style, with my head on a surprisingly comfortable log.

Hours later Freddie woke me up and we set off back to our hotel and the spartan chalet. It struck me as bizarre that Freddie, with everything he had, was still excited at the prospect of sleeping on the floor simply to try the Japanese way of life. There was a certain simplicity to it all and the night's sleep we eventually got had an earthy feel to it. Next morning, on the way over to the hotel, we called in on Joe. His chalet was just as basic as ours but fractionally bigger, which did not please Freddie.

Although Freddie wanted to try the Japanese way of life, his enthusiasm for the country didn't quite extend to wanting to learn the language. He was never interested in speaking other languages; his attitude when abroad was 'I speak English, that's all I recognise.' Even after living in Munich for two years he hadn't picked up more than a smattering of German, although he did pick up a lasting habit of pronouncing some of his Ws as Vs. During our trip to Japan Freddie spoke only two words of Japanese – *domo* and *mushi, mushi.* He'd say them whenever he was excited during our stay but had no idea what the words actually meant; he'd just picked them up because he liked the sound of them.

Our next stop during the visit was Osaka, where we headed for a department store which Freddie hadn't stopped talking about since we left Garden Lodge. It was built almost entirely below ground level, and even the subway passed through. They sold anything and everything but, remarkably, although we must have walked every square inch of the place, Freddie didn't buy a single thing. There was one part of the shop Freddie wanted me to see and he led me there: a large koi pool. He was besotted with them and I could see why. They were magnificent fish.

When we got back to Tokyo that evening, again by Bullet Train, we watched the television news. Freddie fell silent. That afternoon it had been discovered that the tracks on which the Bullet Train ran were dangerous. Freddie always liked to avoid any kind of danger. If he had known about the train he'd have cancelled the visit or insisted on another form of transport.

One of Freddie's passions was fine antique porcelain, and he'd got to hear of a man in Chiba who had a museum filled with priceless pieces. So he asked Misa if she could arrange a private visit. The museum was a good two-hour drive out of Tokyo. As we left the hotel, there was, as always, a handful of patient fans waiting in the lobby, armed with small gifts for Freddie. We chatted to them before setting off.

Freddie hated long car journeys and soon became bored. Then he spotted a McDonald's sign. 'I'd love a hamburger,' he said, so we were diverted into the drive-through for quarter-pounders with chips.

By the time we reached the museum, the fans who had seen Freddie off at the hotel were there before us. 'How the hell did they do that?' Freddie asked, and went to talk to them again.

We started at the museum with a ritual tea ceremony, after which we were shown around the collection of porcelain by the owner. The museum was crammed with pottery of every colour, from tiny, delicate bowls to giant vases twice the height of a man. Even Freddie admitted that these would be too big for him to ship home. As well as porcelain, the museum contained rare works of Japanese art and prints. And there was glorious lacquered antique furniture, including an antique kimono stand, which looked like a small, delicate bedframe stood on end.

When Freddie was shown some beautiful Imari plates he tried to buy them at once, only to be reminded that nothing in the collection was for sale. Everything Freddie saw there he'd have liked to buy, so he kept asking them to sell him this or that. He was determined to keep trying, just in case they changed their minds! At the end of the visit the owner signed a catalogue for Freddie; luckily it was in English, so he could read it on the long journey back to Tokyo.

That night we went out for supper with Misa to a restaurant similar to Tokyo Joe's, where everything was cooked at the table. When we arrived, a Japanese wedding reception was underway, and the bride and groom were posing for their photographer. Freddie looked on spellbound by the bride's fantastic costume. She was wearing a colourful silk kimono decorated with the most elaborate embroidery.

Misa had mentioned to Freddie that some Japanese bathed in sake, the potent rice wine. He quizzed her over what was done, then, at the first opportunity, despatched Joe to buy a large bottle of cheap sake. Freddie ran a bath, poured in all the sake and the two of us jumped in. The alcohol in the sake may have had astringent qualities which were doing us good, but Freddie and I came to the conclusion that a sake bath wasn't something to do a second time. But he did like to quip to friends from then on: 'You go into a sake bath sober and come out drunk!' Freddie was always adventurous, eager to try something at least once – just as long as it wasn't dangerous.

Freddie badly caught the shopping bug again and bought ashtrays by the score. At times what I witnessed in Freddie was panic buying. It was as if he was petrified that the shop would run out of stock before he had made enough purchases to feed his craving. Freddie could shop for England.

Then he discovered a shop in Nagoya with thousands of terracotta *hibachi*s, in all colours, old and new, piled from floor to ceiling. Freddie was still looking for one patterned with a specific shade of old Japanese blue. The search for it had become a running gag. In every shop we entered we'd inspect the *hibachi*s meticulously. So, as always in this shop, we scoured the shelves in earnest, systematically working our way around the store, Freddie's beady eyes checking and discarding every *hibachi* in turn. At one point I was down on my hands and knees combing under the shelving for more. Flabbergasted and laughing, Misa couldn't believe her eyes – she'd never seen such a performance. But what she didn't understand was that Freddie was a perfectionist.

In the end we found what we were looking for. Rummaging around on my knees I found exactly the right blue overlaid with a rich yellow colour. His face lit up the second I showed it to him. 'Is there another one?' he asked. I gasped. Back I went on my hands and knees looking for another, but it turned out that there was only one, and Freddie bought it.

The next shop we went to made beautiful ceramic bowls on the premises, with rich glazes in red and gold. Freddie commissioned two bowls to be made, with his name written inside in Japanese.

Then we went to see an extraordinary lacquer-work collection brought together by one of Japan's Living Treasures, a select title given to Japan's top living artists whose works are of such high quality that they have to be shown publicly before they may be sold. Freddie fell for many of the lacquered pieces and promptly tried to buy the place. The organisers were apoplectic with concern – the work had to be exhibited before anything could be sold, and this was only a sneak preview. They talked excitedly between themselves in Japanese and even Misa seemed a little perturbed by it all. If Freddie managed to buy these things, getting them out of the country wouldn't be easy since works by a Living Treasure were so highly regarded. Freddie finally agreed that he would get his purchases only when they'd been on public show. But they would be shown with a sign saying, 'With the kind permission of Mr Freddie Mercury, from his private collection'.

Within an hour Freddie had spent over half a million pounds. He bought a large reddish brown screen, with falling leaves on one side and koi the other, and three or four other pieces including a cat just three inches high, finely lacquered and polished.

Next day we went out shopping with Itami and our lady interpreter. We called into the Cartier shop and Freddie bought a lighter and two pens. As soon as we got outside, he took out one of the pens.

'Here, this is for you,' he said, passing it to the interpreter, 'as a thank you for looking after me.' She flashed an enormous smile. When we got back to the hotel and the two of us were alone, Freddie gave me the Cartier lighter and the second pen.

Another memorable outing was to see some Kabuki – traditional mime and dance theatre. Freddie loved this very Japanese form of theatre with spectacular costumes and highly stylised acting and stage effects.

'That's what I call theatre,' he said, back at the hotel.

Towards the end of our stay in Japan Misa went to a speciality chicken restaurant. I couldn't make it. The night before, we'd eaten in a small restaurant, and when I got up that morning I wasn't feeling well. It was mild food poisoning and the best thing to do was to stay in bed all day, with Freddie fussing around me like a Jewish mother. Freddie had never seen me unwell before and was reluctant to go out for supper with Misa and Joe because he didn't want to leave me alone. They did go, though, but Freddie spent most of the time wanting to get back to see how I was.

Next morning I still felt ill. Freddie insisted that the days I was laid up wouldn't be allowed to curtail my holiday and he arranged for us to go into extra time, booking later flights back home. 'If you're not well now we're not going to spoil the trip,' he insisted. 'You're going to get your full holiday.'

Misa arranged for a doctor to examine me and write an employer's sick note, in Japanese. Then Joe rang the Savoy in London and explained that I was ill but I'd be back at work a week later. Freddie stayed in the suite with me for the next few days, running around like a mother hen. He would sit next to me on the bed and throw his arms around me as I lay there feeling hopeless.

When I was back on my feet again we used most of the

time for some last-minute shopping. Freddie had already bought a sensational red kimono and we'd hunted in vain for a really good antique stand for it, like the one at the museum. Eventually word got back to us that someone had at last found a lacquered stand and we sped off to look at it. 'Yes, I'll have it,' Freddie said as soon as he saw it.

As a thank you present for caring for him so well, Freddie knew he wanted to give Itami a Samurai sword. He asked Itami to take us to an armoury shop where Freddie bought two swords. Once outside the shop, Freddie surprised Itami by handing over one of them to him. The other was for Terry back home. Freddie also bought a chest of drawers to ship home for Phoebe. And he had a fabulously expensive leather dress made to measure to give to Mary.

It had been a very romantic trip. Freddie didn't need to ask if I had enjoyed it all, the happy expressions I'd worn on my face for three weeks had said it all.

Although we had reached the end of our holiday in Japan, the best part was yet to come: over the coming months Freddie's prize purchases would arrive at Garden Lodge. Miraculously nothing went missing, although a few pieces were broken – most notably the bowls he'd commissioned with his name painted inside them.

We flew back from Tokyo via Alaska, where we had to wait for six hours. Freddie dreaded it. He guessed that the first-class lounge would be closed and that the public waiting rooms would be filled with the weary, impatient or drunk. And he was right. Then, to add a little more to his misery, our connecting flight home was diverted via Munich, where everyone was made to wait for another four hours. By the time we got to Heathrow we were on our knees with exhaustion. We were in no condition for an unpleasant surprise, but when we had cleared customs we were ambushed by a Fleet Street reporter and photographer gleefully throwing into Freddie's face an Aids-scare story.

Under the headline 'Queen Star Freddie in Aids Shock', the *News of the World* had alleged that Freddie had been 'secretly tested for Aids' by a Harley Street clinic under his real name, Freddie Bulsara. The results had showed conclusively, according to a bogus spokesman for Freddie, that he did not have the 'killer disease'. The tasteless story was a flyer – rubbish from start to finish. It even closed by claiming that Freddie and Mary were living together in Garden Lodge.

Freddie flipped. Why had no one from the Queen office in London raised the alarm and alerted him to the story?

'Do I look like I'm dying from Aids?' Freddie told the reporter. He said he had no idea what anyone had been saying and was clearly annoyed at what he called 'such rubbish'.

'It makes me feel sick,' he said. 'Now go away and leave me alone.'

On the way back to Garden Lodge, Freddie was still angry. 'Nice to be back home,' he said sarcastically. But then his face changed. There were more important matters to take care of – he was about to be reunited with our two cats, Oscar and Tiffany.

Freddie gave me a unique souvenir of Japan to go with such magical memories – a gold disc. It was the disc he received for clocking up 100,000 sales in Japan of the Queen album *A Kind of Magic*.

'And I bet you never thought you'd own a gold disc!' he joked when he gave it to me. He was right.

5

YOU'RE FIRED

'Do I Look Like I'm Dying From Aids? Fumes Freddie,' screamed the headline in the *Sun* on Monday, 14 October 1986, which was heralded as an 'exclusive'. Freddie was furious.

He said he hadn't been tested, as the papers had suggested, but the story did make him very edgy for a few days. He was clearly on his guard and for the next few days he seemed preoccupied by the story. Usually Freddie ignored any press speculation, but this time the press seemed to have struck a nerve. I guess that he had secretly harboured doubts about his own health, as before we met he'd done more than his fair share of living the fast-lane life of a successful rock star: all sex, drugs and rock and roll, with a string of one-night-stand strangers.

The day the *Sun* ran the story I went back to work at the Savoy, to my humdrum routine at the barber's shop. The day didn't go well. I was to learn, to my horror, that the concession had been sold. I met the new owner, but wasn't very impressed with him and was even less so when he appointed his brash little brother as manager. Life at the Savoy began to get rocky. The new management tried to change the business from an old-fashioned gentlemen's barber shop into a trendy cut and blow-dry place. My life at work was fast becoming unbearable, but at least I had Freddie and Garden Lodge to come home to.

For Christmas that year, Queen had agreed to release an album of live versions of many of their hits, called *Live Magic*. They had also agreed to take the best part of a year off to give them each a chance to recharge their batteries as well as pursue solo projects.

Their decision prompted stories in the press that they were on the brink of splitting. Stories to that effect were constantly circulating but they were never true – far from it. Sometimes when Queen worked together I could tell from Freddie's mood that there had been arguments, but these occasions were rare and only to be expected. In the heat of the moment each of them may at some point have said they were leaving, but it was never meant to be taken seriously. They were four highly creative artists; being temperamental from time to time went with the territory, and each would hold out for his own views. When they did get badly wound up they would soon work out ways to defuse the situation and, when needed, Freddie could be the most diplomatic peace-maker.

With so much time suddenly on his hands I thought Freddie would want to go out clubbing, but quite the opposite happened. Like me, he became a stay-at-home. We began to lead a very quiet life together at Garden Lodge. Most Saturday evenings Phoebe and Joe went out and left the two of us cuddled up on the sofa watching television. Some nights we'd even be in bed by ten o'clock, though that never meant Freddie got up any earlier the following morning. Freddie liked to have a cup of tea in bed around eight in the morning, then doze for an hour or two before getting up.

At home Freddie loved being surrounded by photographs of everyone close to him, most in silver frames. The grand piano in the lounge was covered in forty or so – pictures of me, Joe, Phoebe, Mary, Barbara, Peter Straker and, of course, the cats. Freddie and I also had photographs either side of our bed.

One night in bed I was flicking through an old album of photographs of my family. Freddie sat next to me and pored over each picture. In particular he liked one black-and-white picture of me as a young boy with my family.

The next night he produced a new silver frame he had bought. 'This is for your family photo – and I know just where it's going,' he said. He stood the picture on a small circular table in the bedroom. It would always be the first thing he saw when he got up.

Paul Prenter was one of the Family as far as Freddie was concerned. He was a long-standing friend who had worked for Queen as a manager for about eight years but been made redundant. To help Prenter out, Freddie had asked him to work for him on some of his solo projects. Towards the end of 1986 Prenter seemed fairly down on his luck, so Freddie decided to give him a great time. He invited him to stay for Christmas and New Year at the flat in Stafford Terrace. And as he was broke, Freddie gave him money so he could go out as much as he wanted over the holiday.

The Saturday before Christmas was grey and overcast, but Freddie was in a sunny mood. He told Terry to get the car ready; we were going shopping at Harrods. Freddie decided it was to be a shopping expedition for expensive perfumes and after-shave lotions, but nothing else. The perfume department at Harrods was soon in consternation, with Freddie adding bottles of every shape and size to his order. He had assembled enough to drown half of Knightsbridge. But then there was an embarrassing moment.

Freddie handed over his American Express card with a flourish and the smiling assistant scurried away to get the huge sum sanctioned, only to reappear looking decidedly uncomfortable. 'Excuse me, sir,' she said to Freddie, 'but you're over your limit. Do you have any other identification?'

'I'm Freddie Mercury,' said Freddie Mercury.

'Yes sir,' she countered. 'I know that, but American Express don't.' The transaction was refused and Freddie was not pleased. Freddie never understood the meaning of the word 'no'. He was great like that. Joe, Terry and I pooled our cash to pay for the stuff in the meantime.

Among the reservoir of scents Freddie bought that day was a lake of Lagerfeld eau de cologne for me; it was the only stuff I wore. The huge bottle made the one on my bathroom shelf look like a free sample. Freddie also gave me a presentation pack of the complete Lagerfeld range, which I still haven't managed to use up even though I've worn it every day since.

Christmas 1986 was an altogether more lavish affair than our first at Garden Lodge. On Christmas Day we welcomed to our home Mary, Paul Prenter, Trevor Clarke and someone who had by now become one of the family, Peter Straker; in all about twenty of us sat down to Christmas lunch. As the dining room was too small we laid two tables running the length of the lounge. After lunch we duly began sharing out the mountain of gifts beneath the tree. I gave Freddie a silver tissue box cover I had found in a little antique shop just around the corner from the Savoy.

Then on New Year's Eve we had a party at Garden Lodge which both our guests and most of the neighbours would always remember. I'd bought fireworks for Guy Fawke's night but had not used them, so we decided we'd let them off to see in the New Year, 1987. Phoebe and I spent most of the day setting the fireworks up in the garden; I placed hundreds of sparklers in the stone urns either side of the front door. As midnight approached, Phoebe and I got to work. I used a blowtorch to light the sparklers. Our firework display lit up the sky and our neighbours cheered and applauded with us at each burst of colour overhead.

For my thirty-eighth birthday a few days later Freddie wanted to give me a piece of jewellery, a chunky gold bracelet. I knew it wasn't my sort of thing, but he disagreed. So we went off to see some in Cartier's, in Bond Street. Fortunately they had none in stock. Instead our eyes fell upon two incredible rings which had been commissioned but not bought: the smaller one was an 18 carat gold signet ring with a platinum top. I tried it on but it was way too big. We aborted the shopping spree.

'Don't worry,' Freddie said. 'We'll get something for your birthday, but you might not get it *on* your birthday.'

Freddie asked me whether I wanted a party at Garden Lodge, but, after the case of the missing vase the year before, I firmly declined. 'No,' I said, 'I'm going to take you out instead.' We went instead to Pontevecchio's, a restaurant not far away from the house in Old Brompton Road, Earl's Court. I also invited Joe, Phoebe, Mary and Peter Straker. It was going to be my treat. Just after I'd called for the bill, however, I felt someone gently tapping my knee underneath the table. I looked down and it was Freddie's hand full of cash. I whispered to him: 'No, I'm paying for this.'

When we got back to Garden Lodge there was another surprise. While Freddie and I squashed up together in a big armchair, opened a bottle of champagne and, for the umpteenth time, toasted my birthday, Joe and Phoebe slipped out of the room. They turned down the lights and reappeared with an incredible birthday cake in the shape of a koi fish with a solitary candle flickering on top.

A few days later I was working in the garden and Freddie came over to me. 'Here's a signed blank cheque,' he said. 'Go and buy yourself a piece of jewellery from Cartier's.' So I returned to Bond Street, picked out the ring I'd tried on with Freddie, and asked them to make it smaller.

When I got home Freddie wanted to know what I'd bought as my birthday present.

'That ring we saw,' I told him.

'Lovely,' he replied.

On Valentine's Day we both sent each other red roses delivered to Garden Lodge. In bed that night Freddie was in a romantic mood; he could always be much more romantic than me.

'I love you very much,' he said.

'I know,' I said.

'Do you love me?' he asked.

'Yes, I love you,' I said.

At the end of February Freddie was releasing his solo single

'The Great Pretender', a cover version of the Platters' hit. He recorded it at the Town House Studios in west London, and worked on the project with Mike Moran, whom he'd first met on Dave Clark's musical *Time*.

The night before the video shoot, Freddie asked me to cut his hair. After that I would cut it every couple of months right up until he died. He'd sit on a chair in the dressing area in the middle of the bedroom. Freddie always left it entirely to me how I cut his hair, and, though we were surrounded by mirrors, he never once glanced into them to see how I was doing. I tended to give him a slightly tighter, more traditional trim than he had been used to previously, but he never complained.

'Whatever you think is best,' he'd say.

Freddie never dyed his hair black – it was natural. He had a bald patch on the crown but never asked me to disguise the fact. He knew there was no point.

Freddie invited me along to watch 'The Great Pretender' video being made after I had finished work at the Savoy, as it promised to be a great deal of fun. He was right. When I arrived the place had a party atmosphere and the loudest screams of laughter were coming from the dressing rooms. They'd been filming all day and now Freddie, Roger Taylor and Peter Straker were getting into drag. Freddie had shaved his moustache off, Terry had shaved his arms with an electric razor and someone else had shaved his chest. When the three of them got into their frocks and started prancing around, the studio erupted into hysterics. I was in tears. I'd never seen Freddie in drag before and he was camping it up like crazy.

Just as funny, Debbie Ash was there to be filmed sitting in an armchair while Freddie jumped on top of her. During the clinches the two of them couldn't keep straight faces and kept cracking up instead. So did everyone watching.

Filming didn't end until about two in the morning, and only then did Freddie tell me how the day had gone. He said that when he'd arrived, hundreds of cut-outs of himself had been set out on the studio floor, but they were not to his liking and so he rushed around adjusting each one. Such things usually had to be left to the unionised studio technicians, but in Freddie's case they made an exception. They knew that he was the boss and would do as he liked.

When it was eventually released, at the end of February, 'The Great Pretender' gave Freddie his highest solo hit. He was extremely pleased about his success, so much so that out of the blue he gave the three of us at the house, and I think Mary, too, 'a little bonus': another cheque for each of us to buy ourselves something special.

The same month Freddie flew to meet opera singer Montserrat Caballé for the first time. During the Magic Tour he'd told Spanish television he was only there in the hope of meeting her, and it transpired that she had been watching the programme. She arranged to meet him in Barcelona, and he'd flown over with Phoebe, Mike Moran and Jim Beach. The two great singers met in a private dining room at the Ritz Hotel.

Freddie said he'd had absolutely no idea what to expect except that Montserrat was prone to tantrums. She turned up late, and Freddie introduced himself by handing her a cassette and spluttering: 'Here, I've got this for you to listen to.' On the tape was 'Exercises in Free Love', a song he'd written with Mike Moran. Montserrat liked the demo tracks and said she would be happy to work on an album with Freddie. He came home on cloud nine.

A week or so later Caballé was in London and Freddie invited her to a working supper at Garden Lodge. It was to be just her, Freddie, Mike Moran and Jim Beach. Freddie discovered what she liked to eat – fish and pasta – so salmon was on the menu. She arrived in an evening gown, and as she walked through the double doors into the lounge she almost tripped.

'Oooh, shit!' she squealed in a tiny, giggly voice.

I was introduced to her before slipping off to bed for an early night. On stage Montserrat looks enormous, but a lot of it is due to the large, flowing gowns she favours. In the flesh she didn't look nearly as big as I was expecting. And far from being awkward in any way, she was delightful: very modest, very camp and very giggly.

Montserrat was only intending to stay for a light supper as she had an early flight the following morning, but in the end she left well into the early hours. As the coffee arrived, she, Freddie and Mike Moran began an impromptu concert around the piano. I fell asleep to the dulcet tones of one of the world's greatest opera divas camping it up with one of the world's greatest rock voices.

A week later Freddie and I were off to Covent Garden to hear a recital by Montsy, as Freddie called her. Princess Margaret was the guest of honour and Freddie and I sat in a box. At the beginning of the interval I jumped up to make a dash for the Crush Bar, but Freddie grabbed me.

'Princess Margaret is here,' he said. 'We have to wait for her.'

I didn't know the protocol, but Freddie did. He was an ardent royalist who adored the Royal Family. The only member of the Royal Family he got to meet was Prince Andrew – and Freddie had promptly invited him to Heaven.

As the curtain rose on the second act, Montserrat walked out on stage and Freddie was spellbound. Then, at the end of the performance, for an encore, she came on accompanied by Mike Moran. She announced she was going to sing a song 'written by two great new friends of mine', adding, 'and I believe the other is in the audience tonight'.

Freddie was really surprised. His hands shot up to his eyes and he started laughing, with an expression of total astonishment on his face. The spotlights swung on to Freddie, his face cupped in his hands, and the audience rose to their feet clapping wildly. So Freddie stood up and acknowledged the applause, and sank back into his chair. He listened transfixed as Montsy performed 'Exercises in Free Love'. At the end of the evening we went backstage to meet Montsy, and then took her back to Garden Lodge for supper.

Later that week, when Montsy arrived in the studio to work

with Freddie, things didn't go quite the way she expected. She thought that to record with Freddie she only had to fly in, sing a few songs from sheet music and leave, but she hadn't reckoned on Freddie's unique way of working. He hadn't written out any of the music for her in advance. Instead he was going to ask her to try something, then keep reworking it until they found the exact effect he was after.

He told her: 'Puccini and all these other composers are dead. I'm alive, dear.'

With that, she accepted his odd way of recording. He proved a hard taskmaster. Later she admitted that in those sessions Freddie got more out of her voice than she knew she was capable of.

On the day Queen were to receive the Ivor Novello Award for their outstanding contribution to British music, Freddie and I had a terrible argument. It didn't last too long but it put Freddie in enough of a bad mood to call me 'a bloody Irish witch' as we left Garden Lodge for the ceremony. By the time we got home Freddie was all cuddles again and I put his hostile outburst down to nerves. When we got into bed that night, he apologised for the row. Then we kissed and made up.

'You're just a big softy at heart,' he said. I was, and I think he found it an attraction; although I appeared to be very tough, behind the façade I was actually as gentle as a lamb.

Before Easter I went home to Ireland to visit my family. I'm sure my family suspected I was gay, although I'd never said anything and I never mentioned I was Freddie's lover. I stayed with my mum, who didn't have a phone, so it meant I had to walk four miles to the nearest phone-box to ring Freddie. The day before I was due to fly back I rang Freddie at home. He asked when I'd be back, and there was an urgency in his voice which made me suspect something was wrong.

'The doctors have just taken a big lump out of me,' he replied. I asked him to tell me more, but he said he couldn't over the phone; he'd tell me when I got home.

'Well, don't worry,' I said. 'I'll be home tomorrow.'

My immediate reaction was that Freddie was exaggerating a little. If he was feeling low, he had a habit of sounding dramatic over the phone to win extra attention from me.

Next day, when I got back to Garden Lodge, Freddie was in our bedroom. As I lay in bed with my arm around him, Freddie cuddled up close and told me what he couldn't tell me the previous day.

He pointed to a tiny mark on his shoulder, no bigger than a thumbnail and with two tiny stitches in it. The doctors had taken a piece of his flesh for testing and the results had just come back. He had Aids.

'Don't be ridiculous,' I said. I couldn't believe it: the doctors had to be wrong. 'Who did this test?' I asked. 'Come on, we'll go to somebody else.' We had to get a second opinion.

'No,' said Freddie. 'These guys are the best available.' It was true, Freddie could afford the best and would accept nothing less.

'If you want to leave me I'll understand,' he said.

'What?' I asked.

'If you want to leave me and move out of Garden Lodge I won't stop you; I'll understand,' he said.

'But I love you,' I said. 'I'm not going to walk out on you – now or ever. Let's not talk about it any more.'

Freddie looked up at me and we hugged very tightly. The consequences of what he'd just told me never really sank in. It was something I was never prepared for, nor had any idea how to deal with. Instead I tried to put it out of my mind as much as possible.

In many ways I was still hoping for a miracle: a mis-diagnosis. Apart from ensuring our sex was safe from then on, I wasn't worried about my own health for a moment. Freddie suggested several times that I had an Aids test myself, but I wouldn't, nor would I give him a reason for my decision.

The truth was that I couldn't see what good my having a test could do. If I was HIV positive or had Aids, I thought there was a real possibility that Freddie might suffer some kind of guilt as in all probability he'd have given it to me. If the test proved negative and I was in the clear, I felt that it would be equally unfair on Freddie, like saying, 'Yah, boo, sucks. I'm all right Jack!' The only thing that mattered was looking after Freddie and trying to keep him healthy.

That was the last time we referred directly to his Aids condition. He never liked talking about his illness and from that moment, if anything came up on television to do with Aids, we would turn over to another channel or switch the set off. It's not that he was unsympathetic to others with the illness; he simply didn't like being reminded of his own fate.

Mary was the only other person at the time whom Freddie confided in about his condition, except for Jim Beach. (He did later reveal his illness to Roger Taylor's partner Dominique after she told him she had breast cancer; he wanted her to know that his was a shoulder she could lean on any time.) Joe was on holiday in America when Freddie told me.

'Should I tell Joe?' Freddie asked me.

'Of course you should,' I said.

Until I discovered Freddie had Aids, we'd thrown all caution to the wind: he and I never had safe sex when we made love. But when I knew of his condition, everything changed and we never had intercourse again without a condom. In fact, condoms were put on Joe's weekly grocery order. Freddie had more tests carried out in the weeks ahead, but they were always done on the quiet and we never spoke about them.

Driven by such devastating news, Freddie seemed more determined than ever to throw himself into work and finish decorating Garden Lodge to his own exacting demands. The rooms and walls, which were still fairly bare, would soon be transformed.

The koi pool in the garden was finished and ready to take fish. To try it out I'd bought a dozen or so goldfish and golden orf, but they were so tiny you could hardly see them. Terry learned of a fish wholesaler in Enfield, Middlesex, who stocked koi and Freddie and I set off one night to look at them. The man told us a new cargo of koi was expected from Japan in a few days and he agreed to let us know the moment they arrived so that Freddie could have first refusal. A few days later the phone rang: the fish had landed. We dashed to the wholesaler. Because of a hitch at customs, we arrived before the fish did. When the precious koi arrived, about fifty of them in all, they were gently lifted from the carriage boxes and placed in holding tanks. Most of them were about 18 inches long and would grow to almost twice that length.

They looked magnificent and Freddie was mesmerised. Then he asked how much they were, and was told between £75 and £2,000 each.

'OK,' said Freddie. 'Give me a good price on the whole lot.'

Without blinking, the wholesaler worked out the sum on his figures and Freddie agreed to buy them all for £12,500. The fish man wanted to call at the house to check whether the pool was suitable. When he did, he insisted we install a mechanical filter. Otherwise, he said the set-up was ideal.

The fish should have been held in quarantine for a minimum of two weeks at the wholesalers, but as soon as the filter was fitted they were delivered to Garden Lodge. The fish soon became the new centre of attention when friends came to visit. We used to make a big thing of Sunday lunch, which became something of a tradition. Usually six or more people turned up late morning for drinks and we'd sit down to eat around two in the afternoon. Lunch would last until four or five, and then the rest of the day would be spent lazing around in the house or garden. The main ingredient was always laughter.

On 4 May Freddie was devastated by another story about him in the *Sun*. And so was I. After all that Freddie had done for him, Paul Prenter had stitched him up.

'Aids Kills Freddie's Two Lovers', it declared, and the story was run across three pages. Tony Bastin, from Brighton, and John Murphy, an American airline steward, had died from the disease in 1986. And Prenter claimed that Freddie had called him late one night and poured out his fears about Aids.

The feature also named me as his lover. My immediate thoughts were of what my family back home in Ireland would make of it. I was due back for a visit, and if word was out that I was the lover of someone so famous they would certainly be disappointed to hear it third-hand from the press. It was something I'd certainly have preferred to tell them in my own time.

When I got home from work that day Freddie and I talked about Prenter's kiss-and-tell. He couldn't bear the betrayal. He couldn't believe anyone who had been so close to him could behave in so mean-spirited a way.

We later learned that Prenter had been paid about £32,000 by the paper for his story. Freddie never spoke to him again after that, and he was also frozen out by Elton John, John Reid and others.

For the next few days there was more in the *Sun*, and at each episode of Prenter's story Freddie became angrier. Prenter sold the paper several photographs of Freddie posing privately with various lovers, such as my predecessor Winnie Kirkenburger, and these were thrown over two pages under the heading 'All The Queen's Men'.

Prenter told the paper in great detail and at great length about Freddie's wilder days with drugs, when he'd regularly shared lines of cocaine with Rod Stewart and David Bowie, sometimes laid out on gold discs. Prenter also revealed that Freddie and disc jockey Kenny Everett had ended their friendship after an argument over cocaine.

Freddie had indeed fallen out with Everett. Apparently, at one get-together Everett had claimed that Freddie was helping himself too freely to his hospitality. But really Freddie said it was the other way around, Everett had taken advantage of his generosity. They never patched things up, and Everett didn't come to Garden Lodge once while I lived there. Even when we went to gay clubs in London, if Everett was there the two of them never spoke to each other. (When Freddie died the papers ran made-up stories of Everett visiting his bedside regularly until the end.)

Speaking to my former boyfriend John Alexander about the trouble Prenter had caused, I learned that Prenter had been bitchy behind my back over Christmas. John had had a run-in with him at a party at Kenny Everett's home. Prenter talked at the top of his voice about me, throwing in plenty of barbed remarks for good measure. Eventually John tired of the tirade and challenged Prenter. He asked him just how well he knew me and, as Prenter mumbled an answer, John told him that he was my ex-lover. Prenter shut up and avoided him for the rest of the night.

A few times after the *Sun* sell-out, Prenter rang Garden Lodge, but Freddie wouldn't speak to him. Prenter tried to excuse his appalling behaviour by saying that the press had been hounding him for so many weeks he'd finally cracked under pressure and told them things by mistake. Freddie didn't want to know of Prenter's excuses; he felt unforgivably let down. The saddest thing of all about the Prenter episode was that it crushed Freddie's ability to trust others, except for a select few. He certainly made no new friends after that.

I often felt sorry for Freddie. For all he had – the money and the success – he could never live a normal life. He couldn't walk down a street or go shopping without being stared at, a pet hate of his.

Feeling bruised by Prenter and the *Sun*, Freddie decided he needed to get well away from them both and we flew to Ibiza for a week's holiday. Joe, Phoebe and Terry came too.

At airports we would adopt a specific formation procedure to shield Freddie; it only took a few fans to spot him, and the next thing we knew we'd be engulfed by a small crowd. If nothing else, they could be time-consuming incidents. So I always walked ahead of him while Joe, Terry or Phoebe flanked him either side. Freddie would walk along with his eyes glued to the floor to avoid all eye contact.

It seems unlikely, but for the man crowned the world's most flamboyant and outgoing rock performer, Freddie really was an excruciatingly private person. If he was caught unprepared by fans he would get terribly embarrassed and say to us under his breath, 'Get me out of here!'

Another thing he would whisper to us from the corner of his mouth always amused me. If we were out in public and he needed the loo he'd say two little words: 'Pee! Pee!' One of us would escort him to the nearest lavatory and hang around to make sure he could pee in peace.

Also accompanying us to Ibiza was something which from now on went with us whenever we travelled outside Britain – a small medical trunk. This had everything from paracetamol tablets and plasters to Freddie's treatments for Aids. The only thing the trunk never stocked were syringes, which were usually supplied locally.

On that trip to Ibiza we stayed at the remote and luxurious Pike's Hotel, a five-hundred-year-old former farmhouse. We'd been there only a few hours before Freddie nicknamed me St Francis of Assisi because of the way the cats and dogs roaming the grounds of the hotel kept running up to me for attention.

By day we all flopped around the pool sunbathing, while by night we headed off to Ibiza's gay bars and clubs. But even there the *Sun* was on Freddie's tail, and their photographer also snatched a photograph of him looking overweight as he played tennis.

Freddie developed a bad wound on the bottom of his right foot. It would dog him for the rest of his life, and eventually made it increasingly difficult for him to walk.

At the end of the trip Freddie and Montserrat Caballé made a surprise appearance at the Ibiza '92 festival to celebrate Spain's staging of the Olympics five years later. The night was wonderfully decadent, held at the lavish Ku Club in San Antonio in front of an elite audience of about five hundred – the Beautiful People of Ibiza, as we called them. Several bands played that night, including Spandau Ballet, Duran Duran, Marillion and Chris Rea. Freddie and Montsy were being saved up to appear as a surprise at the very end.

As usual, I went out among the audience on my own. When the last band came off the stage there was a feeling of anti-climax. Then Freddie and Montsy strolled on together and the crowd erupted. As soon as the first chords of 'Barcelona' struck up, everyone fell silent and every hair on my body stood on end in anticipation. The crowd didn't know what they were in for. While Freddie and Montserrat were singing 'Barcelona' in public for the very first time, the crowd remained absolutely silent. You could feel the pride the song was instilling in them all. Some even shed a few tears.

At the end of the song the audience exploded into applause. Some jumped in the air, waving their arms; others took off their jackets and threw them towards the stage. I overheard a group of young Spaniards saying excitedly: 'This is the new Spanish national anthem!' Then the sky lit up with one of the longest firework displays I've ever seen.

After the show Freddie really whooped it up, first at the Ku Club, then on to Pike's for a whopper of a party. 'Barcelona' had been such a success with the crowd that it made him feel as if he'd won first prize at everything. Several of the Olympic committee so liked the song they vowed it was going to be their anthem for the Barcelona Games.

Back in London, Freddie and Queen were renegotiating their contract with EMI for their next album and tensions had been running high. I came home from work one day and I could sense something was drastically wrong. Joe was standing by the sink in the kitchen and Freddie was sitting at the table looking very stern.

'And you're fired, too!' Freddie snapped at me.

'Pardon?' I said.

'You can't sack Jim,' Joe told Freddie with a gloriously smug expression.

'Why not?' he snapped.

'Because he doesn't work for you!' he said.

'Oh, no he doesn't, does he?' Freddie replied. Then he sat quietly for a few seconds before bursting into laughter. Apparently Freddie, in a foul mood, had sacked all his staff on the spot. Then, at a stroke, he reinstated everyone.

Although Freddie couldn't sack me, I came to discover I did not have much job security at the Savoy. Things at the barber's shop were coming to a head. I'd started telling some of my regular clients that there was a chance I would be leaving, although I had no idea where I'd go next. By mid-July I'd had enough. When I'd done my last trim of the day I phoned the owner of the shop and asked to see him, but he was too busy. 'Fine,' I told him. 'As of 4.30 this afternoon, I'm finished.' He didn't ask me why, but asked whether I would work a month's notice. I said I wouldn't.

I rang Freddie at Garden Lodge to tell him what had happened. Joe answered and told me he was in the dining room in a critical business meeting with Jim Beach and others. He'd given strict instructions not to be disturbed. I insisted Joe got Freddie to the phone, and told him what I'd done.

'All right, dear,' Freddie said calmly. 'You start working for me tomorrow in the garden. We'll work your wages out when you get home.'

When I got back to Garden Lodge, Freddie was waiting for me. 'Give us a cuddle,' he said. 'Well done! I'm glad you're not going to work there any more.' Then we talked about me taking over from the part-time gardeners. I told him I'd work as his gardener on one condition – that no one, not even he, could interfere in what I was doing or the way I worked. It was agreed. Not only that, I even got a wage increase; he put me on £600 a month *after* tax.

Next day at dawn, before anyone else in the house had stirred, I started my new daily routine out in the garden. Another routine began then, too. Every morning when Freddie got up he started his day by looking out of our bedroom window on to the garden. He'd look for me, wave and call 'Cooee' before coming down for his morning tea.

I soon realised I'd taken on an eight-day job in that garden. Although it was nicely laid-out, it still needed many more plants to build it up and add dashes of colour.

Although I was only meant to work at Garden Lodge, occasionally I would go over to Mary's flat to potter around her garden as well, tidying things up. It was on one such trip that Mary and I spoke for the first time about Freddie's illness. It was always impossible to fathom what Mary was thinking, and I don't know whether she was as shocked at the news as I was. Anyway, both of our voices faltered as we touched on the subject. Although I never mentioned anything to Freddie, Mary and I decided we had to do everything we could to ensure that everyone continued to look after him and that his condition was kept from the press at all costs.

Freddie's condition was soon showing physically. A few large, red marks appeared on the back of his hand and on his left cheek. These were called Kaposi's Sarcoma or KS. He got the first marks neutralised by special laser treatment, and they faded slowly. But the treatment left slight blemishes, so whenever he went out in public he would cover the marks on his face with a little make-up. Freddie also developed a painful open wound at the side of his right calf. We treated it with special preparations to stop the weeping but it would never heal properly.

Freddie always seemed to be more anxious about the kois' health than his own. In August we noticed that the fish had become rather lethargic. Then one morning I discovered two of the smaller ones dead, floating on the surface. We rang the wholesaler who supplied them and he came over to take a look. He told us about several diseases they could have caught, but left without finding an answer to our problems. We were flummoxed.

6

OVERTURES AND BEGINNERS

Barbara Valentin was staying at Garden Lodge in the summer of 1987 and she and Freddie, dreaming up something to do, decided to fly to Austria for five days. I didn't know a thing about their trip, and when the two of them left for the airport I was up the ladder trimming the ivy around the house.

I spotted Freddie looking up in a bit of a huff and he called up to me, though I didn't hear what he said. I guessed they were probably going shopping. It was only when I came down from the ladder and went inside that Joe told me they had gone on holiday for a few days.

Freddie and Barbara were due back the following Sunday, but instead came back a day early, on the Saturday. Freddie sought me out straight away and we kissed. I asked him why he was back so early.

'Because I wanted to be with you,' he said.

And Barbara confirmed that he had been pining for me. 'He really missed you,' she told me.

I never met anyone who enjoyed having a bath as much as Freddie. He had one every day of his life, either when he got up or some time later in the day, and favoured them as hot as possible. He could easily spend an hour soaking in the tub, and sometimes these baths became such a performance that Joe and Phoebe would turn up to watch.

One Sunday after mowing the lawn I went up to change,

and as I walked towards the bedroom I heard the unmistakable sound of Freddie singing in the bath. In the bathroom I saw an image of Freddie I'll never forget. He was in the jacuzzi, entirely surrounded by bubbles. It was the first time he'd put bubble bath in the jacuzzi and, of course, he'd wildly overdone the amount. Once he turned the jets of water on the whole place was awash with foam. I could just make out two eyes and a mouth in the living blob of bubbles, and there was Freddie singing camp Marilyn Monroe and Judy Garland songs at the top of his voice, kicking a leg in the air every so often for good measure.

Although Freddie liked a bath, he wasn't one to spend ages tinkering with himself in front of a mirror. He'd clean his teeth and have a wet shave, but that was about all. Nor did he go in for a selection of soaps and shampoos; he would only ever use the range by Lancaster – wildly expensive, of course.

On many occasions, no sooner had Freddie gone to the bathroom to clean his teeth before bed than he'd come running out screaming. 'Spider!' he'd say. 'You'll have you get it out. I can't do it.'

He was a bit of an arachnophobe: he hated spiders. I'd get up, catch the spider and pop it out of the window. Freddie didn't like spiders, but he meant them no harm and would never ask me to kill one. He liked me to catch it in a glass or a box and throw it outside.

Towards the end of the summer the problems with Freddie's koi took a turn for the worse. His favourite fish, two feet long and deep golden yellow in colour, died. I rang the wholesaler and he returned, this time with a fish specialist. We all followed anxiously to see what the specialist would make of the problem.

Without warning and right under Freddie's nose, the chap slid his knife into the body of the dead fish, gutting it wide open, then said there was nothing wrong with it and tossed it aside. Freddie was distraught and furious at what he'd seen. Unable to offer remedies, the two men left. As the gate closed after them Freddie let fly at me, demanding that I quickly find a fish specialist who knew what he was doing.

I phoned every vet in London and eventually found a man who worked for a vets' group called The Ark. He came to the house and sedated some of the koi, examined their abrasions and gave them medication. And he also made some suggestions about what we could do to improve the quality of the water.

More fish died the following Sunday, so in desperation I contacted London Zoo, but even they couldn't help. Mike Moran eventually came to the rescue. He had a friend who kept koi and knew of a renowned koi specialist in London called Neil Porter, who was such a fanatic that he'd given up his GP's practice to devote himself to them.

I rang Neil at his home and explained the whole sorry story. Then I mentioned that the fish belonged to Freddie Mercury.

'Freddie Mercury of Queen?' he enquired.

'Yes,' I replied.

'Well, I charge £60 for the call out fee,' Neil said.

'That's fine,' I replied. 'When can you get here?'

He said he'd try to make it that afternoon and, sure enough, he did. He arrived with his equipment, nets, waders and two sons, who were clearly keen fans of Freddie. Neil took fish from the water at random, examined them then took scrapings. These he placed under a microscope. Some, he discovered, were hosting parasites. I asked exactly what we could do to make the pool healthier.

'To start with, your pond filter is useless,' he said. 'It's not actually cleaning the bacteria from the pond.'

He asked where we'd got the fish and I told him. 'I see,' he said, shaking his head. 'Well, the only thing I can suggest is that I come back tomorrow and take all the fish away to isolate and medicate them.' Freddie agreed, and they were all sent away for months.

While the fish were being treated I had to arrange for the new filter to be fitted and the pool to be modified.

I consulted Freddie about it at each stage, explaining what had to be built or installed, but he was always the same about such things: if I was convinced something needed doing, then I didn't have to ask him about it. 'Fine,' he answered. 'Do it. Don't tell me about it. If you think something needs doing, just do it.'

Next to Garden Lodge was a small street, Logan Mews, and backing on to the wall to the right of the house were two small houses knocked into one with an adjoining garage. The houses had once belonged to Garden Lodge and Freddie had first refusal should the property ever come up for sale. That year the house went on the market for £300,000 or so. Freddie made the owner an offer he couldn't refuse: he would pay the full price by cheque, but as soon as it was cleared he wanted immediate vacant possession.

Freddie handed him the cheque with the memorable words: 'Right, now fuck off.'

No sooner had Freddie put many of the finishing touches to Garden Lodge than he started a whole new home-making project at Logan Mews. And so, suddenly the koi pool and the newly acquired mews house were both being gutted and refitted at the same time. Teams of architects moved in to plan the rebuilding. The Mews, as it became known, would be transformed from its dilapidated state into a smart new three-bedroomed guest house. It was clear that Freddie had many things he wanted to achieve before his illness caught up with him. He wanted to leave a little bit of paradise on Earth.

He also decided to build a conservatory next to The Mews. He sketched out his ideas for an unusual double-domed building and commissioned a company to build it. They'd never seen anything like it, but agreed to make it exactly to Freddie's specifications. It arrived in kit form, and when it was finished it looked wonderful.

In September we returned to Pike's, the secluded country hotel in Ibiza, for another holiday. We travelled in style, flying by private ten-seater jet. With us were Joe, Phoebe,

Terry, Peter Straker and the *Daily Express* reporter David Wigg. Brian, Roger and John and their families were taking a holiday on the island at the same time.

While in Ibiza, Freddie was due to celebrate his forty-first birthday and he planned an almighty bash at Pike's, co-hosting the party with John Reid, whose birthday was a day or so later. The grateful Spanish government and its Olympic Committee, still humming Freddie's 'Barcelona' anthem, were picking up some if not all of the tab.

I don't know if Freddie could swim. I certainly never saw him do so. He seemed afraid of the water. We went out on a boat trip with hotel owner Tony Pike one afternoon and I discovered that Freddie was quite nervous. As soon as we were under way, though, he forgot his worries about drowning and thoroughly enjoyed the day. To put him at his ease further, we opened a magnum of champagne.

Back on shore, drama flared when Freddie discovered that John Reid was pulling out of the party. Freddie was furious. Special fireworks had been commissioned for the night and the grand finale was a vast firework frame which would light up with the words: 'Happy Birthday Freddie and John'. Freddie ordered that preparations for the party should go ahead as planned, including arrangements to fly out eighty guests from London in a privately chartered DC9 and put them up in hotels all at Freddie's expense. (Everyone had such a good time that it was said the flight over was almost as memorable as the party!)

On the day of the party, as we lounged around the pool at Pike's, John Deacon came to me. It was clear that Freddie was no longer able to hide the fact that he was becoming seriously ill. John had noticed some marks on Freddie's leg, the only clue betraying his condition. John directly but discreetly asked me what they were. I passed them off as nothing of importance. 'He's allergic to the sun,' I said, 'they're sunspots.' It was left at that. I put a brave face on it and hid my feelings so that John would not suspect that something was wrong. From that birthday, I knew I was entering my final few years with Freddie.

As well as the British guests imported especially, all of Ibiza turned up for that party. The grounds of the hotel were decorated in transparent coloured paper, running from the hotel courtyard via the buffet tables to the pool. That balmy night perhaps a thousand people poured into Pike's to enjoy Freddie's unstoppable hospitality. The heat played havoc with the Gaudi-inspired chocolate birthday cake – it had melted. Instead, an enormous flat cake was made which was so big it took six people to carry it. 'Barcelona' was emblazoned in giant letters across it.

As the fireworks exploded overhead, each one was saluted in turn by the wildly appreciative crowd. Then at the end the final firework frame was detonated, revealing the shortened message 'Happy Birthday Freddie', and a deafening cheer went up.

Freddie spent the first half of the party outside, mingling, but eventually he slipped back into the hotel to hold court in one of the drawing rooms, entertaining friends as they drifted in and out.

The party was still in full swing when some bright spark almost caused catastrophe by setting fire to the coloured paper decorating the grounds. The stuff was highly flammable and soon a wall of fire shot between the pool and the forecourt, where I was standing. A great flame shot past my face. The fire was brought under control before anyone was injured and, with the exception of a bit of scorching to the hotel's walls, no serious damage was done. I discovered later it was one of the British guests who had caused the fire. Freddie was very angry about it and took it as a personal insult that someone had behaved so badly.

In Ibiza, Freddie gave one of his rare interviews to David Wigg of the *Daily Express*. When we got home Freddie saw Wigg's article in the paper and sighed. 'Look at this,' he said, 'I give them the cream of a story and what do they print? Sour milk.' Wigg later apologised for the way the paper had used the interview, adding that once written it was out of his hands and an editor had chopped it around beyond recognition.

Freddie was doing some chopping and changing too. The Mews was being completely transformed. He became preoccupied with how to decorate it. He decided on some antique ceramic tiles for one of the bathrooms, so we flew to Madrid on a last-minute shopping spree. We found an antique shop with some tiles on display, but Freddie couldn't find what he was looking for.

'Do you have any more?' he asked the owner.

'We've got floors of them,' she said. She then escorted us to every floor, each stocked to the ceiling with tiles.

When we got to the top floor, however, there was an entirely empty wood-panelled room. Freddie looked puzzled.

The panelling contained a succession of doors and behind each one there were old master paintings. When the woman opened the door to reveal an El Greco, Freddie instantly fell in love with it. The picture was a portrait of a man, possibly a self-portrait, and it seemed to leap from the canvas.

'Is it for sale?' asked Freddie. Everything there was, including the panelling. The El Greco cost about £750,000, and Freddie wanted it. But he hit a stumbling block.

'It's catalogued by the government as a painting of national importance and cannot leave Spain,' she said.

Freddie came away disappointed. For days he talked of nothing but that painting, and back at Garden Lodge he contacted one of the Spanish Olympic organisers to see if there was any way he could pull a few strings to allow him to take the painting out of the country. However, he was told the rules could not be broken, even for him.

But that wonderful El Greco picture wouldn't go away. Freddie made a special trip back to Madrid to see it again and he became enamoured all over again. He looked at it in silence for about ten minutes. Then he looked at me.

'Maybe I'll just have to buy a house in Spain, so I can see it whenever I want,' he said. As we flew home he seriously discussed this plan. A few days later he'd given up on the

idea and set his sights on things he wanted to buy closer
to home.

In October Freddie and Montserrat Caballé released the
'Barcelona' single. The record company wanted to make
a video to promote the single, so Montsy flew in for
the filming session in London. On the day of the shoot
Freddie's white-cell count dropped dramatically and his
doctors advised against him working. But Freddie felt time
was of the essence and he was determined to get in as much
work as possible before he was forced to give up; *nothing*
was going to stop him making the video. He insisted on going
ahead as planned.

Freddie's next solo project with Montsy, recording an
entire album of new work together, gave him great strength.
She'd fly in to London to join him in the studio for the
odd afternoon or evening when her globe-trotting schedule
of concerts allowed.

Around October she came over on a flying visit with
her assistant – her niece, also nicknamed Montsy. Freddie
arranged to take the two Montserrats, me, Phoebe and
Mike Moran for supper at the exclusive and ultra-expensive
restaurant Maxim's. But the restaurant did not live up to the
occasion. Everything was wrong about it. It was so crowded
it looked as if they'd started accepting coach parties. The
background music was awful and very loud. And when
Freddie ordered a bottle of the only stuff he liked – vintage
Crystal champagne – they didn't have any.

During the evening, Freddie and Montsy Snr discussed
the format of their album and planned when they could
work together next. Freddie picked a day and she turned
to Montsy Jnr.

'Where am I supposed to be then?' she asked.

Montsy Jnr took out the diary, looked up the date, then
said: 'You're in Russia giving a recital that evening.'

'Oh,' she said. She looked at Freddie, flicked her wrist back
and said: 'Cancel it!'

Freddie's mouth fell open. 'You can't cancel,' he said.

'Yes I can,' she said. And she did. Freddie was flabbergasted by her attitude and dined out on the story for months.

A little later, after we'd finished eating, I was smoking and Montsy Snr leaned over to me.

'Jim, can I have a cigarette?' she asked. Freddie, still a smoker himself then, didn't approve and he tried to intervene.

'You mustn't smoke – it will ruin your voice,' he told her.

'No, no, no,' she said, lighting up. 'I occasionally smoke.'

Freddie found it difficult to believe an opera singer would risk her voice by smoking.

Freddie's collaboration with Montserrat Caballé was such an enormous success in charts all over the world that it caused her to be mobbed by Freddie's fans. She told Freddie she was absolutely astounded by how well the record had done, and said that for the first time in her career she had been mobbed by screaming teenagers when she went through an airport.

I went to Town House Studios many times to be with Freddie and Montsy while they were working on their album. Everyone else watched in raptures but, ever the Philistine, I got a little bored and sloped off to the kitchen for a drink. There I was introduced as 'Freddie's gardener' to Martha Brett, one of the studio staff. She was a bubbly woman who I had met before a few times.

'Would you like a drink, Jim?' she asked.

'Yes, please,' I answered. 'Let's have a glass of wine.'

One glass led to two, and two to three. Then we opened a second bottle. At some stage Terry ran into the room to find me.

'There you are, Jim,' he said. 'Freddie's looking for you.'

'Tell him I'm down here with Martha,' I demanded.

'But he wants to go home,' Terry explained.

'Well, when I'm good and ready,' I slurred. I was usually the one hanging around the studio waiting for Freddie; this time the roles were reversed. I carried on drinking with

Martha. Half an hour later, Terry reappeared. Freddie was still waiting.

'I'd better go this time, Martha,' I said. Freddie wasn't used to waiting for anyone, and I was surprised how he was becoming more patient. His illness was taking the drive out of him, out of being in control of those around him. Now he really needed us, he was less demanding.

One night in the bedroom a week or so later Freddie and I argued about the wedding ring I had bought him. We had been out clubbing and his habit of hiding the ring from the people around him began to annoy me. He seemed too embarrassed to wear it, and I was beginning to feel like a part-time partner.

'Every time you go out of the house you take the bloody thing off. Why?' I said.

Freddie said nothing and slipped the ring on. Then he kissed me and we got into bed. After that night Freddie always wore his wedding ring and it never came off his finger again, even when he washed.

From then on the relationship felt on very solid ground, even though we still had our occasional minor quarrels. Whenever Freddie talked to me about Garden Lodge he always referred to *our* home, and he always told me he wanted me to feel it was as much mine as his.

'It's your home, too,' he'd say.

I'd agree with him for an easy life, but I don't think I ever believed it. It was certainly *our* home while he was alive. I tried not to think what I'd do and where I'd live the day I found myself once more alone in the world without Freddie.

As winter encroached towards the end of 1987, I started to find myself with little to do in the garden. Out of boredom one day in October I decided to take driving lessons. None of us at Garden Lodge drove because, with Terry around, we didn't need to. I saw the idea as a challenge; a little diversion.

I booked a trial two-hour lesson with the British School of

Motoring in Kensington High Street and one morning, before anyone had stirred, I slipped out of the house.

When Freddie got up he looked out of the window as usual, but couldn't see me. He asked one of the cleaners: 'Where is he?' but she didn't have a clue. He hated not knowing where everybody was at all times.

When I finally walked through the gate, he was waiting.

'Where the fuck were you?' he asked.

'I've decided to take driving lessons,' I said.

'What do you want driving lessons for?' he asked.

'No reason, really,' I said. 'It's a bit of a challenge to get me out of the routine of gardening, gardening, gardening while it's quiet. Besides, it's nice to know that if I pass my test I'll always have it.'

He thought about my answers and gave his blessing to the seven weeks of lessons ahead of me.

I don't know what possessed him, but for Christmas 1987 Joe wanted to give Freddie two kittens. I think Freddie suggested to Joe that Garden Lodge was such a big place he wouldn't mind a few new feline faces around the place to add to Oscar and Tiffany. And if one of them turned out to be a tortoiseshell, so much the better. As early as October Joe started searching for a tortoiseshell kitten, and the last port of call was the Blue Cross Animal Hospital in Victoria. He found two perfect kittens there, one with the right tortoiseshell markings, the other with a dark brown coat.

Joe rang to say he was on the way by cab with the two kittens and Freddie started strutting around impatiently. They arrived at Garden Lodge in carriers and once Freddie saw them he was in love. The tortoiseshell was fat, fluffy and lovely, while the scrawny brown kitten was the sorriest of sights. And he had the puniest of squeaks.

Freddie doted on the pair and after a few days named the tortoiseshell Delilah and, rather than the obvious Samson, the other one Goliath.

'Goliath. It'll fool everybody,' he said. 'They'll automatically think Samson and Delilah.'

One day he was working at Town House Studios, laying down tracks for the *Barcelona* album, when pandemonium broke out at Garden Lodge. Freddie treated the cats like his own children. He would constantly fuss over them, and if any of them came to any harm when Freddie was away, heaven help us. During the day the cats had the run of the house and grounds, and at night one of us would round them up and bring them inside. But that night Goliath was missing. Phoebe, Joe and I ran through the house looking for him, frantically opening cupboards and drawers. Then we combed the garden, but we couldn't find him there either. We widened the search to the roads around the house. Still no Goliath.

We knew that if Goliath wasn't waiting with the other cats when Freddie got home, he'd go completely berserk. We kept searching and searching, but by the time Freddie arrived home, shortly before midnight, Goliath still hadn't returned.

We owned up right away. 'We don't know where Goliath is. We can't find him anywhere,' Joe told Freddie.

From Freddie's look we knew that his day at the studio hadn't gone well. This was all he needed. Worried by what might have happened to the kitten, he was close to tears. He ran around the house and garden calling for Goliath. He asked where we'd searched and suggested other places. We were sure we'd looked everywhere.

Freddie became frantic, and in deep despair he hurled a beautiful Japanese *hibachi* through the window of the guest bedroom. It was the *hibachi* we had spent all our time in Japan searching for so diligently.

When Freddie calmed down we talked about what else to do. Joe suggested putting-up 'lost' posters in the neighbourhood, and Freddie said he would offer a £1000 reward.

I went out into the garden one last time calling for Goliath. Then I heard a car pull up in Logan Mews. I heard a front door open and close, then the tiniest of squeaks. I flew out of the house in the direction of the sound. Goliath was crouched under a car, shaking.

I picked him up and went into the house. Freddie was over the moon. For five minutes or more he poured his attention on the kitten, cuddling and stroking him. Then, like a mother, Freddie scolded the cat, shouting and screaming at tiny Goliath for leaving Garden Lodge. The dark ball of fur just sat there, listening calmly to Freddie's outburst and purring loudly.

Whenever I was beavering away in the garden, Goliath would jump up and sit on my shoulder, purring in my left ear while watching me work.

Delilah was another story; she became the little princess of the house. Of all the cats at Garden Lodge, Delilah was Freddie's favourite and the one he'd pick up and stroke the most often. When Freddie went to bed, it was Delilah he brought in with us. She'd sleep at the foot of the bed, before slipping out for a night-time prowl around Garden Lodge.

Delilah was a spoilt cat and depended on Freddie for everything, even protection from the other cats. They would gang up on her and she would run into our bedroom – it was a cat sanctuary. In many ways the cats were Freddie's children and we all thought of them that way. The slightest feline sneeze or twitch and he'd send them off to the vet for a check-up. And we were old-fashioned when it came to having to have sex in total privacy. Whenever Freddie and I jumped on each other in the bedroom to make love, he would always ensure that none of the cats were watching.

That year we had Christmas lunch with Joe and Phoebe at Mary's flat. Mary prepared a lovely meal with all the trimmings, and after lunch we flaked out watching television, then exchanged a few small presents brought over from Garden Lodge; the main presents wouldn't be opened until we returned to the house.

As he did to everyone, Freddie gave me a cheque along with my present. He had pinned it to a card which he signed with love, thanking me for looking after him throughout the year. I gave him a salt and pepper set in Waterford crystal. New Year's Eve was a quieter affair than usual, with only a handful of friends invited to Garden Lodge. Freddie was noticeably slowing up as his illness took its inevitable toll. But we went about our everyday lives, pretending for Freddie's sake that everything was normal.

On 2 January I received a letter telling me the date of my dreaded driving test later that month. On the morning of the test I sat with Freddie and Mary. 'Well,' Freddie said, 'I was going to get you a leather jacket for your birthday, but if you pass your test I'll help you buy a car.'

I said: 'Don't be ridiculous! I hadn't even thought of getting a little banger.'

I took the test and, to my amazement, passed. I couldn't wait to get back home and tell Garden Lodge my news. An hour later I arrived home. Freddie was sitting in the lounge, anxious to hear the news.

'Well?' Freddie asked.

'I've passed,' I said. I was still in a state of utter disbelief.

'Well done!' he cried and jumped up to give me a cuddle.

That night Freddie laid on an impromptu party and told the guests why we were celebrating. Silly little presents turned up all night, including the kind of joke sun-visor which usually identified 'Kevin and Sharon' types as driver and passenger, except mine read 'Melina and Jim'. The names were the wrong way around, making Freddie the driver. There was little chance of that ever happening, though he did tell me he'd once had a driving lesson – just one. It lasted no more than ten minutes. He met the instructor, got into the car, stalled the engine, got out and declared: 'I can't be bothered with this.'

A couple of days after I passed my test, Freddie, Joe and the others were sitting around in the kitchen. Terry came in through the garden with a twinkle in his eye. Freddie had secretly asked him to scout around and find me a car. Freddie called me into the kitchen. On the table were some glossy brochures for a Volvo 740 GLE estate. 'Here, pick a colour,' said Freddie. He was serious.

Mary objected to Freddie buying me this particular car.

She felt it wasn't wise for my first one to be brand-new. I thought she was talking a lot of sense. But Freddie would have none of it.

'For God's sake,' he said to her. 'It's his birthday present. He gets a new car.'

The next day Freddie gave me a cheque for the deposit on the Volvo and Terry ran me to the garage. I was so excited; who wouldn't be? We went through all the colours and the various options, and I settled on a metallic charcoal-grey colour with a sunroof and black leather upholstery.

Later in January Freddie reunited with Brian, Roger and John at Town House Studios to work on a new album, *The Miracle*. Freddie was pleased to get back to recording with the others again. He had several ideas buzzing around in his mind that he wanted to work on.

Freddie and Mike Moran were also working with Elaine Paige's boyfriend, lyricist Tim Rice, on the song 'The Golden Boy' for the *Barcelona* album. Elaine said she wanted to record an album of Queen songs and Freddie said he liked the idea a great deal. He made a point of taking a close interest in how she interpreted the songs.

Freddie and I met up with Elaine and Tim a number of times. One night Tim took us to Wodka, a Polish restaurant in Kensington which stocked some of the finest vodkas in the world, and Freddie was in his element. He tried several different sorts and by the time we left we were almost on our knees. We got back to Garden Lodge completely plastered.

Roger and Dominique Taylor's wedding was held at Kensington and Chelsea register office on 25 January. Freddie and Mary went along as witnesses while, back at Garden Lodge, Phoebe and I gave Joe a hand preparing a small reception for after the ceremony. It was a happy occasion, and while the guests were leaving Freddie gave me a hug and a kiss.

'Do you love me?' he asked.

'Yes, I love you,' I said. I held him tight and we kissed.

He constantly needed the reassurance that I loved him, and

until the end would now and then ask whether I did. He knew I loved him, but he needed to hear me say it. Even though thousands of fans around the world loved him without ever having met him, the only person he seemed to want to know really did love him was me. His fondness for me made me feel very special. I'd never known anyone want my affection so much, and I was deeply flattered. And I loved him dearly in return.

The night before Valentine's Day in 1988 Freddie and I had an enormous row. I'm not sure how it started, but it finished with the two of us going to bed and barely speaking to each other.

Next morning I got up especially early and left Freddie to sleep on. I drove to New Covent Garden, in south London, and bought sixty Blue Moon roses. They were pale blue, larger than the average rose, with a magnificent scent. They were perfect and Freddie was especially fond of them.

I got home and arranged them in a wicker basket. Then I took them up to Freddie in bed, along with tea.

'Happy Valentine's Day,' I said.

Freddie was still in a bad mood with me and grunted. He seemed to have woken up in the same rotten mood he'd fallen asleep in. I left him to it and went down to start work in the garden.

When Freddie got up in the middle of the morning he moved the Blue Moon arrangement into the hall. Later in the day friends came to visit and they commented on the spectacular basket of roses.

'Yes,' said Freddie, 'my husband did them for me.'

They had pleased him, after all. And that night in bed he told me so. We kissed and made up and he gave me a Valentine card.

The next time I met Monserrat Caballé we were going to Pontevecchio's for supper, with about fifteen of us stretched out over the entire end wall of the restaurant. When the Italian waiters saw who our guest of honour was, they couldn't believe their eyes. As a special treat, after supper

Freddie and Montsy broke into 'Exercises in Free Love' and several other numbers.

After working in the koi pool one morning I went into the kitchen where Freddie was having a cup of coffee.

'What's happened to your ring?' he asked.

I looked at my hand and saw that the Cartier ring he had given me was badly dented and scratched. I had damaged it while shifting rocks in the pool.

'That's why I don't like wearing rings,' I told him. Working out in the garden it could only be a danger. I got the ring repaired, and after that I only wore it on special occasions. I'd keep forgetting to put it on after I finished in the garden.

In April Freddie appeared for the first and last time in a West End musical. He took part in a special charity performance of Dave Clark's *Time* at the Dominion Theatre. All proceeds were going to the Terrence Higgins Trust to help pay for research into Aids.

Freddie's own condition was something that he was still reluctant to talk about with me. I knew he went for regular check-ups to his own GP, Dr Gordon Atkinson, and that he had met a number of Aids specialists. I knew, too, that none of them could bring good news. Freddie's death was inevitable. It was simply a matter of how long he could cling to life.

7

DUCKINGHAM PALACE

In the early summer of 1988 Freddie and I flew off to Ibiza for a very quiet ten-day holiday. Phoebe came too, as did Peter Straker and Graham Hamilton, a stand-in driver since Terry was on leave. Before we left the country Freddie was raising merry hell over the time Volvo were taking to deliver my birthday present. He demanded that the car be there by the time we returned.

Unlike our previous two visits to Ibiza, this trip was blissfully quiet and for the first time we didn't stay at Pike's. Freddie was considerably weaker and wanted to avoid any serious socialising; also, he felt the hotel lacked the privacy he needed now more than ever. To avoid the press, we borrowed Roger Taylor's villa and spent most days flaked out around the pool sunbathing, hidden from prying eyes.

Some days we ventured out. We did some shopping in Ibiza, for clothes and pottery and ceramics for The Mews. And we ate in good restaurants every night. The only thing missing was the comfort the cats brought to him. The first thing Freddie did when we got home to Garden Lodge was to herd up the cats who were waiting for us in the hallway.

Also waiting was the news that my Volvo was ready for collection. Terry went with me to collect it from the garage. Freddie had given him specific instructions to take me right away to drive on a motorway for the first time. By the time I got home I was a nervous wreck.

The first journey Freddie made in the Volvo was when I went to collect him from the studio one night. He was a nervous passenger, constantly upset by my terrible habit of creeping up on the car in front, then stopping very close behind. When I did that, Freddie's knee-jerk reaction was to throw his arm out and grip the dashboard. He was in no danger, but I made sure he always wore his seat-belt all the same. And I insisted that there should never be any physical contact between us when I was driving in case he interrupted my concentration.

On that cautious first journey home with Freddie I crept back to Garden Lodge no faster than 25mph all the way – and the 'Melina and Jim' sun-visor sprang to mind. But I took a different route home from the one Terry usually used and, thanks mostly to empty roads, it appeared to be faster.

'Why doesn't Terry take me down this route?' Freddie asked. 'It's much quicker.'

'Because Terry is used to his route and I'm used to mine,' I said. And the sun-visor sprang to mind a second time.

That year I tried my hand again at breeding some koi spawn. The previous year the fry had all died, but this year about twenty tiny fish survived. Freddie took a great interest in how they were faring and took to one in particular, which looked rather sorry for itself as it had a badly deformed mouth. Freddie watched the koi in the pool for hours. He enjoyed feeding them himself, and most adored those which would take food straight from his hand.

One of the spare rooms upstairs at Garden Lodge was used by Joe as a study and was piled high with his books. Freddie said to me one morning: 'I want you to do me a big favour, which might be a little difficult.'

'Fire away,' I replied.

'You know the little room Joe uses as an office?' he asked. 'Well, could you build shelves for it?'

'I'll have to think about it,' I said. 'Where exactly do you want them?'

'All around the walls,' Freddie told me. 'From floor to ceiling.'

I measured up the room, then headed for the timber merchant's to order the wood. I got the wood home and spread it out in the garden. I designed shelves which would slot together. There were four units in all, to fill two sides of Joe's room.

In the afternoon Freddie asked: 'What are you doing now?'

'I'm making your shelving units,' I replied.

'I didn't mean for you to make them so soon,' he said.

'Well, I might as well,' I answered, shrugging my shoulders. And that kept me busy for the next three weeks. Every so often he'd pop in to see how they were coming along and I'd chase him away.

Terry gave me a hand to install them. Still Freddie kept asking: 'Are you sure they're going to fit?'

They did fit, perfectly. It was the first piece of carpentry I ever did for Freddie. But it was not to be the last.

A week later Freddie searched me out in the garden.

'I've got another little favour to ask you,' he started.

'What?' I asked.

'I've had paint made up to the same colour as the wallpaper in Joe's office. Could you paint the units the same colour?'

Of course I did, and when the shelving was completely finished he came to see them and was over the moon. But, as always, Freddie was only over the moon for a day. Soon he was working out what else was needed in the house.

Shortly after I made the shelves, I damaged my back badly in the pond. I wasn't happy with the positioning of a stone bowl, which was fed by water from a large bamboo shoot resting on rocks.

I waded into the pond in my waders, then tried to reposition the bowl. I moved it, but in doing so pulled my back, displacing a disc and cracking a vertebra in the small of the spine.

I refused to go on painkillers in case I started lifting things which were too heavy. For the next few weeks I had to go to a physiotherapist. After several visits I was given exercises to do. I was practising in the Japanese Room one day, lying flat on my back, when Freddie walked in grinning like a Cheshire cat. He lay next to me on the floor and asked how I was and what I was doing, so I explained.

As I turned over for the next exercise he was facing me. He smiled and said: 'I've got a little present for you.'

I slowly opened the little Cartier box. Freddie had given me a pair of cufflinks.

'What's this for?' I asked.

'Oh, I just wanted to buy you something,' he replied.

'You shouldn't be wasting your money on these,' I said. I didn't wish to sound ungrateful, but that was often what I felt about his never-ending generosity.

He'd buy things on the spur of the moment, perhaps going through a jeweller's catalogue until his eyes fell on something he liked. This time Joe had been instructed by Freddie to go to Cartier's to buy cufflinks for his husband.

Another time I was getting a lot of trouble with insects eating the plants in the conservatory. Whenever Freddie was with me I would plough through gardening manuals trying to work out which creatures were killing the plants. In the end I found the answer: red spider mites, too small for the human eye to see. I bought a magnifying glass to be able to see them. The plants were infested with them.

When I got into bed two days later, Freddie gave me a box. I opened it and there was a beautiful silver magnifying glass and a silver letter opener.

'Well, I want you to be able to see the bugs,' he said.

It was in the autumn of that year, on a particularly dank day, that I met for the first time Freddie's parents, Bomi and Jer Bulsara. They came to Garden Lodge to have dinner with their son. There was a strong physical resemblance to his mother, a little lady with dark, greying hair and a lovely smile.

At the time The Mews and the garden were still a mass of

foundation trenches and mounds of earth. I was in the garden and Freddie brought his mum and dad out with him when he brought me a cup of coffee. He had not told them about our affair.

'If they ask you where you sleep, tell them in the Pink Room!' he said.

A few minutes later, as he showed them around The Mews, I overheard them asking who I was.

'He's my gardener,' Freddie said.

'Where does he live?' they asked.

'He lives here, of course,' he replied.

I didn't get to speak to Freddie's parents that day, but I met them many times after that and we always got on well. I would drive Freddie over to their small terraced house in Feltham, Middlesex, to visit them. We'd both sit down with them for tea in the kitchen.

Mrs Bulsara always got the tea at her own pace – she never rushed around. She was very independent and still drove herself everywhere in her little car.

The Bulsara home was very homely. Freddie had lived there since the family first came to Britain. (They were originally from Zanzibar, and moved first to India before settling here in 1964.) I don't think they kept a bedroom for him there, nor did they have any photographs of Freddie on display. Freddie had once offered to buy them a bigger house, but they said no. They were clearly very content with what they had.

Freddie's dad was very proud of his garden. One day he took me out to look at it. He had a fabulously shaped eucalyptus tree and many beautiful old roses. When we reached the roses he said, with a hint of regret in his voice, that he was sorry the roses were reaching the end of their natural life. I wondered whether he was telling me he knew that Freddie was reaching the end of his life.

I can't remember Freddie telling his parents that he was ill, but as time went on it was difficult to disguise from them the fact that something was terribly wrong. Freddie's physical appearance was beginning to change and he looked

With Freddie in the grounds of Garden Lodge in 1985, the very first time he took me to see the place.

With Freddie in Munich, 1985.

With Freddie and feline visitor Dorothy in Munich, 1985.

With Freddie and Dorothy.

Left to right: Roger Taylor's assistant, Chris 'Crystal' Taylor, with John Deacon and Freddie playing Scrabble on the tour-bus, 1986.

Banana in hand for a pretend microphone, Freddie swanned around excitedly trying out his new regalia the moment it arrived for the 1986 tour.

Freddie's jubilant costume designer, Diana Mosely.

Just as Mary Austin and I posed for this picture, taken during the Magic tour, Freddie leapt on top of me.

Sparring partners - Freddie and me during the Magic tour.

With Freddie in Japan for our £million 'holiday of a lifetime'.

Freddie and me with just one day's Tokyo shopping - probably worth around £250,000.

Misa Watanabe, our Japanese hostess, with Freddie.

Where's my dinner? Freddie hungry for his supper.

At the Geisha school with Freddie. The make-up fascinated him, so did the kimonos.

Freddie at the Geisha school.

A typically comic birthday present - a gardener's apron. Freddie was beside himself with laughter.

The gardener at work in Garden Lodge.

For Christmas in 1989 I gave Freddie a silver cut-glass caviar bowl worth its weight in the stuff.

Boxing Day 1989 in the dining-room at Garden Lodge, wearing matching his-and-his shirts.

New Year at Graham Hamilton's home. *Left to right:* Freddie struggling with a party popper, Mary and our host.

Barbara Valentin and Freddie the night he wrote the song 'Delilah', dedicated to his favourite cat.

The two of us with Barbara Valentin in Switzerland, 1990.

A break during filming for *Breakthru* in Cambridgeshire, Queen's first ever outdoor video shoot.

The last birthday Freddie ever celebrated was in September 1990 - a grand, dressy affair held at home.

Left to right: Mary, Freddie and Barbara during his last lavish birthday supper. I sat opposite.

Freddie's birthday, 1990. *Left to right:* Tony Evans (a friend of Joe's), Trevor 'B.B.' Clarke, Freddie's doctor Gordon Atkinson and Graham Hamilton.

Freddie's last Christmas, 1990, with Joe and his bird.

Collapsing at New Year's Eve - the two of us with Graham Hamilton in 1989.

A typically lavish flower arrangement in Freddie's bedroom. He'd call 'cooee!' to me every morning from that window.

Freddie's flat in Switzerland (the top floor of the building on the right). The last trip we made was in October 1991 and I know that's when he decided his battle against AIDS was over.

Freddie in the spring of 1991, looking frail and thin. This was the last time he posed for a photograph.

Freddie Mercury - My man!

Freddie set his heart on an antique kimono stand - and, Freddie being Freddie, he got one in the end.

The two of us between two sensational Japanese works of art, even Freddie admitted they'd be too big to ship back to Britain!

Singer Peter Straker with Freddie in the kitchen - more than once they stayed up screaming hysterically all night.

Peter Straker and Freddie trying out the new jacuzzi in The Mews.

Gay as a daffodil - Freddie showing off a camp little basket one Christmas to Peter Straker.

What do you give the man who has everything? Quality Street never went amiss - and even played a part in the Christmas decorations.

Travelling in style - for trips to Ibiza and Switzerland Freddie often hired a private jet. *Left to right:* Graham Hamilton, Freddie, Terry, me and Phoebe.

My Blue Moon roses for Freddie on Valentine's Day 1988. 'My husband gave me those!' he told everyone.

A sleepy Freddie, wearing the wedding ring I gave him, sipping the first cup of tea of the day.

Miko.

Oscar.

Goliath in *that* sleeping place.

Romeo - and Freddie.

Lily.

Freddie's favourite cat, Delilah, in
her favourite soft spot.

Freddie loved his birthday cakes, this one with it's
oriental flavour was typically over-the-top.

Winter Wonderland at Garden Lodge - snow on the ground and lights twinkling in the tree.

Freddie's beloved koi - plus the visiting ducks.

Freddie and his people. *Left to right:* Mary, me, Mary Pike (one of the maids), Phoebe, Freddie and Joe.

Phoebe with a birthday cake for Joe - a ski scene, as he was about to head off to the slopes for a holiday.

For my 40th birthday Freddie threw a surprise supper party, and I was given this amazing icing creation - of the conservatory at the Garden Lodge.

Freddie gave me the cake - then I gave him a big kiss.

For Mary's birthday in 1990 Freddie cooked up a feline surprise.

thinner on each visit. Freddie's mum knew he was very ill. I have a feeling Freddie did eventually tell them the truth, but he did not do so in front of any of us.

Freddie went to see his mum every Thursday afternoon for tea, and he rarely came away empty-handed. His mum made wonderful cheese biscuits and packed them into a little lunch-box for him. In fact, in one of the last photographs the newspapers published of Freddie he was outside Garden Lodge with a box of his mum's cheese biscuits under his arm.

That same year I met Freddie's sister Kashmira for the first time when she and her family came to stay for a few days at The Mews. You could see at once that she and Freddie were sister and brother – they had the same big, dark brown eyes. Her daughter, Natalie, was a sweet, boisterous kid and she also had a baby son.

Freddie's family was important to him. Whenever he was away, no matter where, he always made a point of sending cards to his parents and his sister.

He was also in love with beautiful furniture. One day he fell for a beautiful wood and glass coffee table made by a master craftsman. It was made in the Japanese style, which of course Freddie adored. The only problem was the price: about £2000. In the end Freddie thought it too expensive and decided not to buy.

Shortly afterwards he said: 'You could make one of those, couldn't you? If you make one for me I'll pay for it.'

My family back in Ireland are builders and carpenters, so I guessed that if I sent them photographs of the original they could make the frame in kit form; all I'd have to do was order the glass and assemble the wood at Garden Lodge. But then I decided to have a go at the whole thing myself, so I started searching for books on making furniture.

I bought some tools and set to work in the workshop. The first table was about three feet square and made from pine. When the frame was finished it didn't look bad for a first attempt. Next I went to the glazier's and ordered the plate glass. When it arrived, heavily packaged, at the house Freddie got excited. Then he realised my mistake. I still worked in imperial measurements, but the thoroughly modern glazier had gone metric – my confused calculations were incorrect. I'd shrunk my order to a piece of glass just nine inches square.

'Silly fool!' laughed Freddie. I went back to the glazier, who rushed the order. When it arrived this time it fitted perfectly, and Freddie was delighted when he saw the result. But he didn't like the plain pine, so he asked me to paint it a dark reddish maroon. I mixed the paint myself, and in the end spent more time painting the table than I had making it. Freddie derived great pleasure from the fact that I'd made the table especially for him.

We returned to Ibiza for a holiday, and this time Freddie was hyperactive; he just couldn't be restrained. It was 'shop till you drop!' time again. He was particularly looking for ceramics for The Mews, which he'd now decided was to have a Spanish flavour.

Miles out in the country on Ibiza we found a huge place with bulging shelves of ceramics. As we went in, Freddie asked what I thought of the stuff.

'All tourist tack!' I replied flippantly, not realising that the British owner was just behind me. Actually Freddie found several lovely things there, so I was a little hasty. They were glazed terracotta lamps in yellow, one of his favourite colours. Back home, Freddie took the lamps over to The Mews but couldn't find anything to put them on. 'You couldn't make two tables for these to stand on, could you?' he asked.

So I soon got cracking on them. They were made from pine and MDF, medium density fibreboard, then painted and finished off with glass tops. I took them into The Mews and was positioning them when Freddie came in.

'What have you been doing?' he said. 'I haven't seen you for days.'

I pointed to the tables and said: 'Those!'

'You didn't make those, did you?' he said and went over to inspect them.

'Yes,' I replied. 'I did.' He looked at them closely, then kissed me.

Soon he was asking if I'd make an occasional table for our bedroom. I needed a lathe for my workshop, to turn the legs, so Freddie bought me one. The table legs were a nightmare. I tried turning them several times and each time went wrong, so I cheated and bought four thick banister rails. Then I spent a good month French-polishing the table.

When I gave it to Freddie he was thrilled. He said he knew exactly where he wanted it to go – just inside the bedroom door, to put photographs on and to show off a few knick-knacks, too. Making things for Freddie gave me the answer to the question – what do you give the person who has everything? My presents of hand-made furniture became one of Freddie's greatest pleasures.

But my first love remained the garden and making it as special as possible for him. One Sunday I was weeding the lawn just before lunch. Freddie was waiting for the lunch guests to arrive and came over to see what I was doing. Soon he wanted to try digging some weeds out of the lawn as well. The two of us were on all fours looking for small weeds in the lawn. Then the guests started arriving and, one by one, Freddie commandeered them to join us. By the time lunch was ready everyone was on all fours weeding the lawn!

Freddie kept to his word and always left everything to do with the garden to me. He made the odd suggestion, but I retained the power of veto over him. My quest was to keep improving the garden, and each year I would experiment with new plants and new colours. Freddie was always delighted with the results, but as he was the world's most impatient man he expected everything to be in flower after one day of sunshine.

Only once did he manage to get one over on me in the garden. He came to me one morning and asked me to plant an indoor azalea among a bank of outdoor azaleas all the same colour. It would look incongruous, so I refused to transfer it. A little later when I was having coffee in the kitchen, Freddie came in laughing. I knew he'd been up to something, but he wouldn't tell me what. A few days later I found out, when I discovered the newcomer among the azaleas. He had planted it behind my back.

That summer we went to Montreux in Switzerland for a break. Freddie was no stranger to Montreux, for he had often worked in a studio there in the years before I met him. He always rented a lakeside house called The Cygnets, because of the number of swans on the lake you could see from the windows. Freddie nicknamed the place The Duck House and Roger Taylor went one stage further, dubbing it Duckingham Palace. The house was like an elegant bunker, half underground with glass panels all along one side and a stupendous view of the water.

Freddie was very relaxed and I think the clean mountain air did him some good. Montreux felt a much healthier place to live in than London. As in London, we spent most of the time cuddled up on the sofa watching television. We could get out most days for a walk around the lake to look at the swans.

When we got back to London a new addition to the Family was imminent, and Garden Lodge was in a flurry of activity. Mary had found a lovely tortoiseshell cat and although Freddie already had a tortoiseshell, Delilah, the coat of this one was quite different. We all fussed over the new baby kitten, though she didn't get such a warm welcome from the other cats. Goliath was so timid he'd run away if he spotted her, while Delilah would hiss. Oscar and Tiffany simply ignored her.

The kitten was named Miko, and in the end she won over Goliath and even Delilah. We'd come down some mornings to find the three of them snuggled up in the basket together. Before long they were such friends that Delilah would even clean Miko, licking her all over.

Like the New Year, Freddie's birthday party in September was a quieter affair than in earlier years – just a small garden party at the house. Before it started I gave Freddie my present, an antique silver jewellery box.

Among the guests were Roger Taylor and members of his band The Cross, part of his new solo career. The lads from The Cross were fairly rowdy and their slobbish behaviour irritated Freddie a great deal. When they eventually left, Freddie was clearly glad to see the back of them.

'What a pain they were,' he said. 'They're never coming here again.'

Some time later, we went out for supper one night to Pontevecchio's with Mary and Dominique Taylor. Towards the end of the evening a woman came around selling single roses and I bought three. I gave one to Mary, one to Dominique and the third to Freddie. He was terribly embarrassed because I had shown such a public show of affection. But later, in the bedroom, he thanked me for the rose and kissed me passionately.

On 8 October 1988, Freddie and Montserrat Caballé appeared at Barcelona's La Nit Festival to welcome the Olympic flag to the city. They topped the bill of the star-studded gala which included Spandau Ballet, Suzanne Vega, José Carreras, Jerry Lee Lewis, Dionne Warwick and Rudolph Nureyev, who was also dying of Aids. The show was being staged in front of the Son et Lumière Fountains in Castle Square, in the presence of the King and Queen of Spain, King Juan Carlos and Queen Sofia, and their daughter Princess Christina. Freddie and Montsy sang 'How Can I Go On', 'The Golden Boy' and 'Barcelona', backed by the Barcelona Opera House orchestra and choir. But despite the rapturous applause, Freddie did not consider the night a success. He found himself in the nightmare all singers dread – he had lost his voice.

The British press had been flown over and had been promised an interview with him. But on the day of the show, not for the first time, Freddie had big problems with his throat nodules. He was in a terrible state and clearly wasn't in a mood to give an upbeat, in-depth press interview. So reluctantly he called it off. Inevitably this added fuel to the press speculation about Freddie's poor health.

All day Freddie worried about whether his voice would last the show and, with great reluctance, at the very last minute the decision was taken that he and Montsy would have to mime their songs. There seemed no alternative, short of cancelling the show completely. As he got into his three-piece dinner suit and bow tie in the dressing room, a tent backstage, he was the usual bag of nerves.

We had some time to kill before he was on. During one interval Freddie was taken to meet the Spanish royal party, and he returned in a slightly more cheerful frame of mind. And he was cheered further when we met Dionne Warwick backstage. He told me she had been an idol of his since childhood and he ranked her as one of the great female vocalists of all time. He was totally in awe of her.

When Freddie and Montsy stepped out on stage together things at once went terribly wrong. The playback tape was running slow and had to be stopped. Then there was silence as the tape was rewound to the beginning. It was a terrible giveaway and spelt out to everyone in the audience that they were miming.

Freddie was wild about the mistake. He wrestled through the first song, then darted into the wings to wipe the floor with anyone he could find. He was still fuming back in the dressing room after the performance and slammed a large vodka down his throat. He was furious at the sound technicians for letting him down so badly. Wisely, they kept well away from him.

Freddie emerged from his tent in a tracksuit and put a brave face on the catastrophic evening. He had to meet some notables and representatives of the Spanish Olympics committee. And the night ended, as always, with fireworks. 'The Spanish love their fireworks!' Freddie said to me. Back at the hotel we had our own private party. Later, when we fell into bed, he couldn't stop talking about his meeting with King Juan Carlos.

Two days after appearing in Barcelona, Freddie was back in Britain for the launch of the *Barcelona* album and the single 'The Golden Boy' taken from it. Montsy was flying in on the day of the lunchtime launch party, to be held at Covent Garden. There was a story that Freddie had arranged for the album to be advertised on the M4 to welcome Montsy, but it wasn't true. He said later he wished he'd thought of it, and he would have done.

Freddie met Montsy in the foyer of Covent Garden. Joe, Phoebe, Terry and I slipped into the crowds to soak up the atmosphere on the pavement. There were press photographers everywhere; when she arrived Montsy ploughed straight through, scattering them in all directions.

I returned to Ireland for a fortnight to see my family. While I was away Freddie got bored and flew to Munich for a few days with Phoebe and Peter Straker.

I arrived back at Garden Lodge on the Sunday to learn from Joe that Freddie was in a great state about the garden. While I was away a blanket of fallen leaves had covered the garden and Freddie wasn't pleased.

First thing the next day I set about raking them up. Then I was told that Freddie wanted me to join him in Germany. When I got there Freddie had the beginnings of a cold and was in a bad mood. He blasted me out.

'What's this I hear about you not doing the garden?' he demanded. 'It's in a state, a dreadful mess, with leaves all over the place.'

I replied: 'You know I've been to Ireland for two weeks. I can't rake leaves up from Ireland, can I?'

'Well, I just heard that you haven't been doing your work,' he added. Someone around Garden Lodge had clearly been stirring things. Then he calmed down and we all went for supper at the hotel. The plan had been to meet Barbara Valentin afterwards to go drinking in bars in the Bermuda Triangle, my old stomping ground with Freddie. But Freddie didn't want to go out, because his cold had made him feel lousy. Instead, he decided he wanted to turn in early. At first

Phoebe and I were reluctant to leave him, but he insisted we all went to meet Barbara.

We had a great evening. We weren't particularly late, but there was plenty to drink and by the time we returned to the hotel we were all fairly well gone. I fumbled around trying to find my key card and was so drunk I tried to open the door with my Visa card.

Freddie was woken by the terrible racket outside, and went into a great tirade. We made our apologies, but he didn't seem to want to know. Once I was in the bedroom, he snorted: 'I'm not feeling well. You're all out enjoying yourselves and I'm not well. At least you could have had the decency to stay behind.'

'It was offered,' I said. It cut no ice.

He was in a foul mood and I think, looking back, it was because his illness was getting to him. In frustration he was trying to take it out on me. But at the time I didn't realise that and I took it all very personally. A vicious argument followed.

We said some terrible things to each other in the heat of the moment during arguments like these. We'd both say things we didn't mean. They could become a battle of who was going to hurt the other most. This time Freddie had the upper hand.

Then we made up and lay next to each other on the bed. I was crying. For the first time since he had told me of his condition Freddie brought up the subject of his death. He asked me a very odd question, the gist of it being: 'What are you going to do when I die?'

'I don't know,' I said, still crying. 'I can't handle it all.'

'Well, how do you think I feel?' he replied. I looked over and Freddie was crying too.

He cuddled up to me and we cried quietly together, hugging each other tighter for some kind of reassurance. A few minutes later I got up to go to the bathroom and did a very odd thing: I shaved off my moustache.

When I returned to bed Freddie looked astonished. He'd never seen me without my moustache. He knew I loved the moustache so much I thought I'd never shave it off. It was a sort of token sacrifice to show him how sorry I was that he was having a bad time.

We cuddled up in bed and he soon fell asleep. But I didn't. I lay awake crying most of the night, with the thought of Freddie's illness and his inevitable death racing through my mind. What was I going to do when he died? I had no idea.

I often used to cry on my own, thinking about Freddie and his illness during quiet moments at Garden Lodge, but I made sure he never saw me doing it. I'd go to bed and cry myself to sleep. Through the day I tried to put all thought of Freddie's illness at the back of my mind, but in the still of the night it would come back to haunt me.

We got back to London but Freddie couldn't settle for long and soon we were off to Montreux for another short break. Freddie did a lot of window shopping that visit. He was taken with some plain, pure white porcelain in a shop window as we strolled by. He asked me why the porcelain was plain. I didn't have a clue, so the next day I returned to the shop to ask. The man explained that the pieces were unfinished. They were delicately patterned only after the customer had placed their order. I told Freddie what I'd found out.

The man who ran the shop turned out to be a famous porcelain artist called George Misere Shrira and we went back to see him. On closer examination the shop boasted some fabulous pieces of porcelain, including some Limoges pieces made in France. We bought some ashtrays and a few other things, and then Freddie asked whether the man would agree to paint *any* intricate design.

He said: 'Yes.'

Freddie then commissioned from him two large table lamps with imperial designs on them. When they eventually reached Garden Lodge, Freddie was delighted with them. With their usual accuracy, the *Sun* reported that Freddie had bought a thirty-six-piece dinner service.

Back in London we went to Peter Straker's birthday party, held at the Xenon nightclub in Piccadilly. Tim Rice and Elaine

Paige were there, and Freddie also met Fay Treadwell of the Drifters.

As we started getting ready for Christmas and began hanging decorations, I also transformed the garden into something of a Winter Wonderland scene. In the magnolia tree by the gate I hung tiny white fairy lights. Freddie loved them so much that they never came down after that and he asked me to hang some in the other magnolia tree which could be seen from the bedroom window. Time and again I refused.

'It'll be too much,' I would say. 'It'll make the place look like a fairy grotto.'

Like Habitat furniture, I felt that a little went a long way. Less was more.

Inside the house, I had great problems with the Christmas tree. It had been ordered specially, but, once in place and decorated, the needles began falling off. After a few days we had a completely bald tree.

To Freddie it was a huge joke, but I wasn't so happy. It was starting to look pathetic and Christmas was still to come. When I got the supplier to swap it for a healthier one, Freddie teased me that he preferred the other sorry specimen.

In the days before Christmas Goliath started finding unusual places to sleep in. He always made himself scarce when visitors called, and one night as guests arrived he disappeared on cue. But after a few hours he still hadn't resurfaced and Freddie became quite concerned. Had Goliath gone missing again, like the night when Freddie had offered a £1000 reward? We ran around looking for him. I went upstairs but couldn't find him in any of the bedrooms. Then I found him asleep in the jacuzzi bathroom. It was such a serene scene that I left him sleeping and ran down to find Freddie.

'Come on,' I told him, 'you've got to look at this.'

Freddie came up, took one look at Goliath asleep in the marble washbasin and let out a hysterical scream. It became Goliath's favourite spot to take a snooze, on a par with the laundry baskets for comfort.

When Mary arrived at Garden Lodge for Christmas 1988 she took one look at the mound of presents beneath the tree and, joking, picked out the most beautifully wrapped present.

'This must be mine!' she exclaimed.

'Yes, it is, dear!' said Freddie. When she opened it she was suitably astounded. Freddie had bought her a beautiful Cartier briefcase.

Freddie always wanted my present to be a surprise, and that year he went to elaborate lengths to throw me off the scent. Terry had been despatched to buy a camp selection of presents to help me in the garden: *white* overalls, an over-sized pair of wellingtons and a stainless steel shovel. All were parcelled up colourfully and well disguised – even the shovel didn't look like a shovel. Freddie watched as I unwrapped each in turn. He loved my giggly reactions and he exploded in laughter as each spoof present was unveiled.

A little later he said: 'They weren't your real present – that's under the tree.' I unwrapped it to discover a fabulous piece of Lalique crystal, shaped like a cat.

Then I gave Freddie my present to him, also crystal. It was a huge lead crystal and silver caviar bowl. Freddie always liked caviar and offered it freely to his guests.

Freddie always threw Garden Lodge open to his friends on Boxing Day, and that year it was bursting at the seams. Peter Straker was appearing in the musical *Blues in the Night* at the Piccadilly Theatre, and half of the theatre world seemed to follow him to the party – Carol Woods, Debbie Bishop and her then boyfriend actor Nick 'Hazell' Ball and Stephanie Beacham plus her two daughters. One of the daughters was called Phoebe, just like Peter. Nick gave me a ball radio and a battery-operated child's toy – small penguins waddling around a loop-track. That toy kept me and the cats occupied for hours. They'd wait for the little penguins to get to the top of the ski slope, then whack them all off.

8

THE RETREAT

My fortieth birthday in January 1989 was one I wanted to forget, as it reminded me I was getting on a bit. But Freddie took me to the Meridian in Chelsea to celebrate. He said, 'I'm taking you out tonight, as forty is the big birthday.'

Mary came with us in the car and by the time we got there everyone was waiting – Joe, Phoebe, Peter Straker, Dave Clark, Graham Hamilton and his partner Gordon, yet another driver, and John Christie, a singer. Our table stretched along the full length of the restaurant window. And, by happy chance, Eartha Kitt was sitting at the next table with some rather gorgeous young hunks.

'What would you like to drink?' Freddie asked. 'Go on. You can have anything tonight.' He suggested champagne, but I stayed on still wine until the end of supper, when I slipped back bloated in my chair and sipped a brandy. Then Freddie fixed his eyes on me and all the lights in the restaurant dimmed. Waiters wheeled out a birthday cake which was typical of Freddie's wild imagination: a three-dimensional iced model of the Garden Lodge conservatory. I looked around at Freddie and the others in astonishment, then blurted out: 'You bastards!'

I glanced at Freddie's impish look of delight, then I kissed him.

Phoebe's birthday was four days after mine and we celebrated at the Bombay Brasserie, a very plush Indian restaurant in west London. Phoebe's cake really knocked him sideways. It depicted a dramatic scene from *Othello*.

The same month Freddie released his duet 'How Can I Go On?' from the *Barcelona* album with Montserrat Caballé.

On Valentine's Day that year I bought Freddie two dozen roses in an unusual black colour. I arranged them in a vase and placed them in the hallway to greet Freddie when he came downstairs. He came out to me in the garden, kissed me and thanked me for them. A little later, his roses for me arrived.

The following Sunday I was working in the garden when Freddie emerged from the house looking a ridiculous sight. He was wearing the out-sized white overalls and massive wellingtons he'd bought me as a joke at Christmas.

'Now then, what are you doing?' he asked me.

I burst out laughing. He wanted to give a hand and tried helping me with a bit of weeding, but he didn't know what he was looking for. In the end he just got under my feet so I marched him indoors to encourage him to interfere in whatever Joe or Phoebe were doing instead.

Not long afterwards I went to visit my family in Ireland. A neighbour of my mum's, who lived in a bungalow opposite, had put her home on the market for £32,500 Irish punts (about £25,000 sterling). She asked me if I'd take back with me the estate agent's particulars of the property to pin up in Irish pubs and clubs in London.

Coincidentally, back home at Garden Lodge Freddie received a letter from a woman who ran a cat sanctuary. He had made a few large donations to her and she'd moved the operation to new premises, also a bungalow. He held up a photograph she'd sent of the property and studied it assiduously. I ran to fetch a picture of the bungalow in Ireland belonging to mum's neighbour.

'You think that's a nice bungalow. How about this one?' I asked, passing him the particulars. 'Ooh,' he sighed, studying the photograph carefully. 'Is it for sale?' he said. I told him it was.

'Then buy it!' he said, forgetting at first that on a salary of £600 a month it was well outside my range. Then he offered to lend me the money. I thought about it for a moment, but then said I'd rather stay independent and get a mortgage of my own. However, if that failed, perhaps we could talk again about a loan. I stressed that if I did borrow money from him it would all have to be done properly with my weekly repayments docked at source.

I rang mum's neighbour and made an offer on the bungalow. She accepted, but I did tell her that should anyone else come along to better my offer she'd be mad not to take it.

I applied to the Bank of Ireland in Dublin for the mortgage. In the application form I simply said I worked as a gardener for Goose Productions Ltd, with no mention of Freddie Mercury.

We spent most of 1989 between London and Montreux while Freddie and Queen worked in the studio. The first few months were spent putting the final touches to their album *The Miracle*.

Freddie was always interested in Queen's success in Britain and the rest of the world, but in all the time I was with him, he took no interest in how the band were doing in the USA. Queen had done well there, but the Americans weren't too sure what to make of such an uninhibited and flamboyantly gay rock star. He had given up on the country and told me he had no intention of ever returning. The band was so universally popular elsewhere that he said it didn't matter to him.

Not that Freddie disliked America. He owned a sensational Art Deco penthouse apartment in New York in a building so exclusive that his seriously wealthy neighbours usually frowned on rock stars, however famous they were. In Freddie's case they made an exception as he turned out to be a model tenant.

The apartment had sensational views of the Chrysler Building and beyond. Its Art Deco decor and fittings, with lots of mirrored panels, were original, and Freddie had furnished it in keeping with the period.

In all the time Freddie and I were together the flat remained unoccupied. Gerry Stickles, the band's tour manager, was based in America and kept an eye on the property for Freddie. Phoebe would also be despatched occasionally to take a look at the place and stay in it for a few days. On some trips Freddie would ask him to bring back a few small treasures he wanted – a beautiful crystal vase or a delicate porcelain bowl.

One story always trotted out as a so-called exclusive about Freddie's time in America concerned his working with eccentric singer Michael Jackson. They spent only a short time together in a studio, working on collaborations which never saw the light of day because they were never actually finished.

Freddie told me they had worked on a rap number. More memorable for him was an unusual invitation from the singer. Although he had liked Michael Jackson as far as their brief friendship went, he felt he didn't understand Freddie's sense of humour and had even frowned on his liking of cocaine. The most memorable part of the experience was suitably wacky. Jackson offered Freddie an unusual invitation – to visit his llamas. Freddie was dressed, typically, in white trousers, but agreed.

'That was a mistake,' Freddie said. 'When we got there I was up to my knees in llama shit.'

I was flabbergasted one day when, speaking to the Dublin branch of my bank about the mortgage, the man on the other end said: 'I hear you work for Freddie Mercury.' How did he know? I hadn't said a word. I'd done everything I could to keep that fact secret.

Still, it proved the end of my plan to buy the bungalow. I went back to Ireland just before Easter and mum's neighbour began shouting at me. She said she'd had other offers, so I asked her why she hadn't accepted one, as I'd suggested. What with one thing and another, my dream of buying the bungalow foundered.

Mum knew I was disappointed and made a suggestion. 'Why don't you have half of my garden and build your own house? At least then you'll have exactly what you want,' she said. The idea had possibilities, especially as I came from a family of builders. Later that day I bought my mum a new washing machine as her old one had broken. 'That's lovely,' she said, as I wheeled it in. 'That's in payment for the land then!'

When I got back to Garden Lodge, I told Freddie of mum's offer of the land and he was very positive about the idea of building my own place. In fact he said he would help me build the house. So I contacted my nephew Jim Sheehan, a building engineer who'd studied architecture, and we arranged to get the idea to the drawing board.

The same year Freddie decided he would buy a flat in Munich with Barbara Valentin. They would split the cost of the property equally and do the same with the decorating bills; they both had equally expensive tastes. Furthermore, in the event of either of them dying, it was agreed that total ownership would pass to the other.

Freddie seemed to like the idea of sharing something very special with Barbara. She found an apartment and Freddie was enthusiastic about the project for months; then his interest waned. He knew he was unlikely to get any real use out of the flat; he would almost certainly die first. There was no escaping the fact that he was losing his battle against his illness.

Freddie had taken to covering the marks of his KS with makeup whenever he went out in public, but it didn't seem very practical to me. So I suggested he grew a short beard, enough to cover the blemishes, which he did. The beard inevitably made headlines before long.

One day, after working on the plans for the house with Jim Sheehan, the two of us went out for a drink. It was the first day the pubs in England were allowed to open all day, and we celebrated the event with lots of drinks. I got back to Garden Lodge ten hours later, steaming drunk. From then on, with Freddie's encouragement, I often went out to drink on my own. Freddie warned me that I could lose my friends because of our relationship and urged me to remain in contact with them. It was a kind suggestion from Freddie, who had been thinking a lot about how I would manage alone. I guess he knew I'd have to call on my friends when he was dead and I was back on my own again. And I guess he knew that my slipping out for a drink now and then helped take things off my mind.

After several meetings Jim Sheehan and I completed the plans for a rambling three-bedroomed Irish retreat. Freddie pored over them, thinking through which rooms were going where. Finally he approved them.

Then we discussed money. The Bank of Ireland mortgage had fallen through and I was going to have to take up Freddie's offer of a loan. My family's estimate to build the house was £32,000 and Freddie agreed to the amount. The money would be a loan, and Mary would arrange for regular repayments to be taken from my wages.

In May Queen stormed the album charts with *The Miracle* and the single charts with 'I Want It All'. This was their first new material for three years and was long awaited. But even before the records were in the shops Freddie wanted to push on with recording more material.

Queen were dazed by Freddie's eagerness to return to the stresses of the studio. I don't think any of them had thought about going back to recording so soon after briefly coming up for air after *The Miracle*.

But they all said 'Yes' in unison.

The same month, on the 20th, Freddie arranged for us to go out with the band and their partners to possibly the world's greatest restaurant, Freddie Girardet's, at Crissier, near Lausanne in Switzerland. A stream of fourteen delectable nouvelle cuisine dishes were served, accompanied by some equally delicious wines. Brian's girlfriend, actress Anita Dobson, made me laugh when she said: 'I'd rather have bangers and mash!' The bill for the night ran into thousands. Freddie Girardet signed our menu 'To Freddie and Jim'.

Around the same time the same group met up for a quiet

supper near the studio in a restaurant called the Bavaria. That was the night when Freddie admitted to the band that he was not well.

Someone at the table was suffering from a cold and the conversation got round to the curse of illness. Freddie still looked fairly well, but he rolled up his right trouser leg and raised his leg to the table to let the others see the painful, open wound weeping on the side of the calf.

'You think you've got problems!' he told them. 'Well, look at this. Look what I have to put up with.'

Everyone was very shocked but also very sympathetic. Then, as quickly as he'd mentioned it, Freddie brushed the subject aside.

I think the band had all been well aware that Freddie was seriously ill, and his leg that night was the confirmation they had all been expecting.

Back in Britain, the papers reported that Freddie had been in a dramatic accident in the Swiss Alps when his car had spun out of control. The reports were totally without foundation.

However, rumours about his health were stirred up when he gave an interview to the DJ Mike Read for Radio One. Freddie said he didn't want to tour again; he felt he had toured enough and was getting too old to go strutting around stages any more. The truth was that he was getting too weak to take on such a schedule ever again. The press interpreted his remarks differently, claiming that by refusing to tour he had caused another bust-up in the band and that once again they were about to split, this time for good.

'It shows what they know,' said Freddie when I showed him the reports.

Far from being on the verge of going their separate ways, the band was already working on what would come to be thought of as their greatest album. It was *Innuendo*, their last.

While in Montreux one week with Freddie, I picked up some catalogues for beautifully made precision model train sets. The top-of-the-range was a beauty, the gold-plated

Rhinegold. Freddie and I were looking at the catalogues in Garden Lodge when he said he wanted to buy me a model train and it would be a Rhinegold. A stockist near Oxford Street had one for sale and I set off to buy it at once. When I got home I began making a table for it, with miniature mountains and scenery. I couldn't rest the board on its side, as it could get damaged too easily, so it used to be kept on top of Freddie's Rolls Royce in the garage adjoining my workshop.

Freddie's Rolls went back a very long time. He had bought it in the seventies, long before my time with him. Word had it that Freddie signed his very first record contract in the back of a Rolls and it was something he always wanted as soon as he could afford it. Yet he seldom used the car. I didn't go out in it once, though I did drive it in and out of the garage when I wanted to play with my trains. In fact, Freddie preferred to be driven around in a Mercedes.

That summer I flew back to Ireland to apply for planning permission for my house. The plans were duly passed, and I rushed home to tell Freddie.

'I've got the go-ahead to build my house,' I told him.

'That's *our* house!' he said, and from that moment Freddie only ever talked enthusiastically of *our* house. It was never 'yours' or 'mine'; it was always *ours* – just as he always reminded me that Garden Lodge was *our* home.

The video for Queen's single 'Breakthru', released in June, was a first – it was the first Queen video not to be made in a studio. Instead the band were to be filmed hurtling along on the back of a steam train, renamed *The Miracle Express*. A private railway was used for the two-day shoot: the Nene Valley, in Cambridgeshire. A location shoot depends on good weather, so we prayed for sunshine for the two days and, thankfully, got them. They were swelterers.

The location had been kept a closely guarded secret to keep the fans at bay, but they turned up in hordes all the same. The local radio station announced Queen's visit to the whole of Cambridgeshire. When we pulled up at the Nene Valley railway station there were fans everywhere. It all added to the fabulous atmosphere.

While Freddie was filming I commandeered Graham Hamilton, Freddie's stand-in driver, to take me to Cambridge. I had decided to buy Freddie and me some pairs of shorts. Graham and I asked one of the police officers guarding the station how far Cambridge was, and he was more than helpful.

'I'll escort you in,' he said. 'I'm about to go back anyway.'

So I went shopping in Cambridge that day with a police escort.

Even though Freddie was constantly working that year, he still wallowed in his domestic routine at Garden Lodge. Busy as he was, nothing ever escaped his attention.

When the koi started spawning there was so much of the stuff I had to keep pulling it out of the pool by the bucket-load to prevent the adult koi from eating them. This time many young fish survived. The holding tank wasn't big enough for all of them so I had to cull some. While I was doing this I decided to put a small fish I'd bred the year before out of its misery. It was deformed, swam badly and had difficulty eating. I killed it with a quick rap to the head.

When Freddie came into the garden, without being told, he guessed what I'd done.

'Where is it?' he said.

'I've killed it,' I told him.

'How?' he asked. When I told him he hit the roof. He said that if I ever had to kill fish again I must find a more humane way of doing so. On Freddie's instructions I rang the fish specialist, Neil Porter, who sent me special powder to kill the fish humanely.

Getting up one morning in Garden Lodge, Freddie asked me if I could make him another small table for our bedroom – *identical* to the first. My face dropped.

'What's the matter?' he asked.

'Why didn't you ask me to do this when I was making

the first one?' I said. 'Now you'll get different shades of mahogany when they could both have been made from the same cut of wood.'

However, I hoped to be able to reproduce a similar tone with wood dyes. When Freddie found me later in the day, I was measuring up the first table.

'Didn't you draw plans for that table?' he asked.

'No, I didn't,' I said.

'If you drew plans you wouldn't have any trouble at all,' he said. 'All you'd have to do is go back to your plans to make another.'

'Well, I never make plans for these things,' I said. He seemed surprised. His would have been a much more organised approach.

But when I showed Freddie the finished table he was delighted, and from then on the two tables sat either side of the bedroom door, covered in framed pictures and bits and pieces.

Some time later Freddie bought a number of ormolu furniture brasses.

'I've got a marvellous idea,' he said. 'Now I've got all this ormolu brass, let's put some on those two tables you've made,' he said.

'It will ruin them,' I told him. 'These are just plain, simple little tables.'

'It won't,' Freddie insisted. 'They'll work perfectly, I know they will. I know about these things.'

He ran out of the room to find the large bag of ormolu fittings and started choosing which he wanted where. Once they were arranged, they did look good.

Freddie took great pride in the tables and always showed them off to visitors, telling them: 'My husband made them for me.'

I also made a hinged wooden box, just for something to do, and Freddie commandeered it for himself as soon as he saw it. He came into the workshop while I was polishing it.

'What are you making that for?' he asked.

'No reason,' I said. 'I'm just tinkering about.'

'Can I have it for my private papers?' he said.

'Of course, but perhaps I'd better put a lock on it,' I added. I searched everywhere for a lock small enough. In the end I took one from an old sewing machine which had belonged to my grandmother.

When I handed over the box to Freddie he put it on show in our bedroom. But he never used it to store anything. It didn't need a lock after all.

We had some great news at Garden Lodge when Mary announced she was expecting Piers Cameron's baby. So now, during our regular trips to Montreux, baby clothes and toys were also on the shopping list.

During the pregnancy a cruel story appeared in the papers suggesting Freddie had struck a love-pact to 'father' a child for Mary, her child by Piers. It was unfair and untrue. So was the suggestion that Freddie would become godfather to the baby. When the story appeared, Freddie suggested some sound advice to Mary.

'What you should do now, darling,' he said, 'is get a nice photograph of you and Piers and release it to the press.' But Mary preferred to deal with the matter her own way and did nothing.

In August, as the group's single 'The Invisible Man' hit the streets, we had a newcomer at Garden Lodge, another kitten. I spotted it in a pet shop in Kensington High Street, where it sat on its own in the window bawling its head off. It was very big-boned with grey, white and black striped markings. I popped in and asked Colin, the owner, how much it was – £25. I thought it was too much, so I left it and went on my merry way. When I got back to Garden Lodge I told Phoebe and Joe about it.

'If you like the kitten that much, why don't you buy it?' they said. I told them I thought Freddie would go up the wall if another cat arrived. Then I had a change of heart and headed off to the shop. By the time I got there, three women were haggling with Colin over the kitten. They each wanted him, but balked at the prospect of having to buy a £5 cardboard carrier. Leaving the women to fight amongst themselves, Colin called over: 'Yes, Jim, can I help you?'

'How much is the cat?' I asked, although I already knew the answer.

'£25,' he replied. I took £25 from my pocket and gave it to him.

'There you are,' I said. 'The cat's sold. I hope you don't mind, ladies.' And I swept out with the kitten in a cardboard carrier.

The Mews gave us a second entrance to Garden Lodge, so to avoid Freddie I slipped in that way with the cat carrier. I didn't want to have to admit that I'd bought the cat, but blow me if I didn't bump straight into him.

'I've got something here,' I said. 'If you don't like it then I'm going to give it to Anna Nicholas.' Anna was an actress friend of Freddie's who, only a few days earlier, had been asking him where she could buy some cats. I knew she'd be happy to give it a home if Freddie didn't want it.

'What is it?' Freddie asked.

'I'm serious,' I said. 'If you don't like this . . .'

I opened the box and Freddie peeped inside.

'You bastard!' he said. I could tell from the expression on his face that the kitten could stay. He soon decreed that the kitten should be called Romeo.

'He's going to be a very big cat, too,' I added quickly. 'Even bigger than Oscar.' In fact, Romeo grew to be a real bruiser of a cat.

Not long after little Romeo had arrived I got important news from Ireland. The family were ready to start building the bungalow, so I went to Freddie for the money. He filled in a cheque and passed it across to me. When I looked at it I tried passing it back as it was for several thousand pounds more than I needed.

'No,' I told him. 'It's only going to cost £32,000 at the most.'

'But that's only a reckoned figure,' he replied. 'That's why there's a bit more.' He paused for a moment, then added: 'This is a present.'

I did protest, though probably not as strongly as I should have. Actually, it turned out to be such a big bungalow that the money Freddie gave me still wasn't quite enough. I didn't tell Freddie, but I secretly took out a small mortgage for £15,000 to make up the shortfall.

Anyway, encouraged by Freddie, for the next nine months or so I went to and from Ireland for brief visits to see how the building work was progressing.

Each time I set off he'd tell me: 'Take as many pictures of *our* house as possible.' I'd take either the still or video camera and I would show Freddie the latest development when I got back. He wanted to know everything.

From time to time, instead of Joe cooking supper Freddie would send one of us out to buy a takeaway meal. He liked the odd hamburger, but only Wendy hamburgers, or better still fish and chips which we'd eat straight from the paper. Freddie would insist we bought an extra six fish – one for each of the cats – and it was always my job to prepare them for them. To keep Freddie happy I had to take off all the batter and check for bones so none of them would choke.

By 1989 my dreadful, unstoppable snoring was beginning to take its toll on my life with Freddie. It kept him awake. And when I went out drinking it became even louder.

One night I was snoring my head off in bed next to Freddie and he tried turning me over so I would stop. It didn't work. Eventually he got so annoyed that he pushed his knee into my back and it woke me up.

'What are you doing?' I said.

'Snoring!' he growled.

'OK,' I said. 'If it's that bad I'll go into the guest room.' So I got up and left him to sleep in peace.

The Pink Room, our sparsely furnished large guest bedroom, was only a few steps down from the master bedroom. It had a large bed and a big unit, a self-standing triple mirror and a couch so big it had been brought in through the window

– Freddie decreed it was for our house in Ireland when it was finished. Off the bedroom were an en suite bathroom and a dressing area.

My move into the Pink Room was part-time at first. Most nights I'd sleep with Freddie, but if I was likely to snore I crept off to sleep on my own.

That October in Switzerland, Freddie was working with the band and suddenly gave up smoking for good. It happened like this. For most of the year Queen had been working in the tiny Mountain Studios in Montreux where the control room was minuscule. When Brian walked into the room one morning he quickly backed out, complaining that the room was far too smoky for him.

'Right,' Freddie demanded, 'no more smoking in the control room.' It seemed slightly unfair on the studio engineer, Dave Richards, because he couldn't go for a cigarette whenever he wanted. But there and then is when Freddie gave up cigarettes.

Although he'd cut down to milder brands, Freddie often had catarrh on his chest first thing in the morning caused by smoking. He'd get up and start coughing and spitting. In Switzerland he got up one morning and spluttered so badly I told him he had to cut down. Then I lit up myself.

Freddie never missed smoking from that day on. He'd been smoking all his life yet he hadn't become hooked. I was and still am.

Towards the end of 1989 Tiffany the cat was dying of cancer. One morning in October she was clearly in agony and looked as if she didn't have long to live. Before Freddie was awake I took her to our vet, Keith Butt. He came straight to the point: 'Jim, we really should put her down. But I'll leave the decision up to you.'

I left Tiffany with him and went back to the house to consult Freddie. I told him Keith's verdict on the sick animal. Freddie was crushed. Mary arrived and Freddie told her what was going on. We all knew the decision we had to make, and after a few moments Freddie agreed. Mary accompanied me back to the vet's, where Tiffany was given an injection and instantly fell asleep.

'That's it, Jim,' said Mary softly.

Tiffany was cremated and her ashes buried in a little casket, just as Freddie wanted, outside, and exactly in the middle of, the enormous dining room window. It was very touching.

The same month Queen released their latest single 'Scandal'; the B-side was 'My Life Has Been Saved'. The band's next hit, which came out at the end of November, was *The Miracle* album.

That Christmas I decided to make the Rhinegold train set the centre-piece for the Garden Lodge decorations, and I transformed the board into an enchanting snow-scene. Twelve days before Christmas we started putting up the decorations in earnest. I decided the only place my train scene could go was on Freddie's black grand piano in the lounge. I cleared all the photographs away, placed polystyrene blocks on the lid to protect it from scratches, and lowered the board in place. Then I set up the train.

When Freddie went into the lounge I heard him hitting the roof, so I ran in after him. Freddie said he loved the idea of the train-set, but he wasn't at all happy that it was on his piano: it might scratch the lid. I pointed out the lengths I'd gone to in order to protect it, and then he calmed down and said it was fine.

That afternoon he helped me deck the two double doors from the hall with red and white painted twigs from which red and silver balls dangled.

'There's something not quite right,' Freddie said. 'It needs a little *umph*ing.'

'It's got the balls,' I replied.

'No,' he said. 'It needs something else.' He fetched a big jar of Quality Street chocolates. 'Here,' he said. 'Throw some of these up there.' We both agreed they made a big difference.

On Christmas morning, Freddie came to me.

'I'd like you to do something,' he said softly.

'What?' I asked.

'I'd like you to put a little bunch of flowers where Tiffany is buried.'

Boxing Day that year was especially memorable for everyone at Garden Lodge, thanks to a little surprise laid on by Freddie. When we got to the dining table, by each place Freddie had laid a small present of outrageous costume jewellery – a brooch or a trinket – from Butler and Wilson. There was one for everybody – Phoebe, Joe, Mary, Peter Straker, Dave Clark, Graham Hamilton and his boyfriend Gordon. Some got little silver poodles on chains, others tiny golfers or a musical clef. But I got the best of all: an outrageous tie-pin set with a huge, transparent cut stone.

When Jim Beach came to visit Freddie over Christmas he fell in love with my train-set. When he decided to buy one for his son and asked me to set it up for him, I was happy to oblige. Jim was the band's manager, but he was always very much their employee. I got on very well with him, but I don't think he could understand the relationship Freddie and I had; nor did it matter. He knew I made Freddie happy, so that made him happy, too.

The New Year started with Jim trying to find a new record deal for Queen in America. They had been with Capitol for a number of years but weren't happy with their treatment, so the band bought back the rights to their back catalogue in the USA. It put them in a strong negotiating position.

Early in 1990, when we'd had Romeo for several months, Freddie and I were walking into the conservatory, quickly followed by four of the cats. Suddenly Romeo turned on Goliath, Delilah and Miko and starting fighting. I looked at Freddie and called out 'Rambo!'

'What do you mean, *Rambo*?' he asked. 'Watch him,' I said. 'He's attacking all the other cats. He's Rambo.' It was a nickname which stuck.

In Ireland I didn't know what to do about the flooring in our bungalow. In the end I asked Freddie what I should do. He asked what the options were and I mentioned white

Canadian maple for the lounge, which I could get cheaply through a family contact.

'Find out how much it will cost!' he said.

Two weeks later Freddie returned to the subject. 'Have you found out how much the maple will cost?' he asked.

I told him the price I'd been quoted.

'OK,' he said. 'I'll pay for that. It will be a present to you.'

Soon we were back into a hectic schedule bouncing between Mountain Studios, Montreux, and Metropolis Studios in west London, where Freddie and the band were laying down tracks for their final album, *Innuendo*. For months we ate, slept and drank Innuendo.

In February Queen was honoured with an award for their outstanding contribution to British music by the British Phonographic Industry in a ceremony at the Dominion Theatre. Freddie didn't look well even though he was caked in thick make-up for the television cameras.

After the ceremony, a party was held at the Groucho Club to celebrate Queen's twenty-one years together. It was a celebrity-packed event, with guests including George Michael, Liza Minnelli, Barry Humphries, Michael Winner and Patsy Kensit. Freddie held court at a table at the back of the club. When Rod Stewart arrived Freddie introduced me to him as 'My man, Jim'. I was reminded of Freddie's joke about wanting to form a band with Rod and Elton John, called Teeth, Nose and Hair.

Martha Brett accompanied me to that party and was very dressed up. She was a huge Rod Stewart fan. While Freddie and Rod were talking she kept staring at him. Then Freddie in turn started staring at me.

'Who's that you're with?' he asked. 'I don't know her.'

'That's Martha!' I said. From the Town House Studios.'

'Is it?' he asked. He looked a bit harder and then burst out laughing.

Later in the evening an extremely imaginative cake was wheeled out. It was of a Monopoly board, but all the property squares were Queen hits.

Before he became front-man for Queen, Freddie studied at Ealing College of Art in west London. He had long given up painting, but one day he got a sudden urge to try again. One of us was sent to buy up a small artists' supply shop for brushes and materials.

For several weeks he would lose himself for hours at a time in his sketching and painting. He tried painting a portrait of Delilah but, like so many of his pictures, it was never finished.

He only ever finished two pictures, for Joe and Phoebe, and they came about quite by chance. Freddie was flicking through a Sotheby's catalogue one afternoon and stopped at a modern portrait for sale, drawn in straight lines.

'I could do that!' he said.

He grabbed a sketch pad and a minute or so later he had finished. He held it up and it was a perfect copy.

'Can I have it?' Joe said.

Freddie signed it and gave it to him. Then Phoebe asked for the same again and after a few minutes Freddie had dashed off another copy.

Freddie loved art. He favoured Japanese and Impressionist paintings and had something of an aversion to modern art. If he came across modern pictures in auction catalogues he would scoff; his least favourites were massive expanses of canvass painted a single colour or featuring a couple of straight lines.

'What's the point of it?' he'd say. 'It's not art.'

A few days later we went to Montreux. We arrived in the early evening and there was an absolutely stunning sunset falling over the lake. Freddie wanted to take a photograph of the two of us, standing in that romantic sunset, but we didn't have a camera. He became agitated. He had set his heart on the romantic picture.

'Don't worry,' I said. 'We'll get a photograph taken.'

It is one of my greatest regrets that we never did get around to it.

One of the first things Freddie liked to do when he arrived

in Montreux was look at the swans on the lake. He referred to them as 'my' swans and as soon as he'd seen them he felt he could quickly settle back into the Swiss way of life.

That day, after strolling over to see his swans, Freddie sat at the water's edge and was inspired to write a song called 'A Winter's Tale'. It was a Christmas song about Switzerland and life in the mountains. It was never heard. Freddie recorded the song, I'm certain of that, but the tape has never seen the light of day.

Freddie usually arranged to start work around noon. He was suffering from a drastic loss of weight. Still, he insisted on getting up by himself in the morning, and he took no longer than usual to dress and have his cup of tea before setting off for the studio.

Increasingly he would ask Terry to stop somewhere on the way to the studio. 'I want to get out and walk from here,' he'd say.

The first time it happened Freddie appeared to be deep in thought. He asked Terry to park by the lake. He wanted to be alone for a few minutes and he walked very slowly to the opposite side of the lake to the swans. He stayed with them for a few minutes, then slowly walked back to us.

'That's it,' he said. 'I've had enough. Time to go to work.'

After a while Freddie found walking very difficult. I gave him a walking stick, but he wouldn't use it. He agreed to try it just once, but that was the only time. Nor would he use a crutch. Managing without help was part of his strength. He had to keep doing it on his own for as long as he was able.

'I'm going to keep going until Mother Nature says, "No, you can't go any further",' he said.

One day back in London Freddie and I headed out with Graham Hamilton and his boyfriend Gordon because Freddie wanted to buy some glasses from Thomas Goode's, in Bond Street. He also bought a canteen of cutlery for our bungalow in Ireland. I told him I was popping out for a cigarette but went straight to the Lalique glass shop in nearby Mount Street. I knew the woman there as Freddie was one of their regular customers. The manageress came over.

'I want to buy a little surprise present,' I told her. She knew at once who it would be for.

'How about a cat?' she suggested. The cat she had in mind was glass and mounted on a plinth. It was ideal. I bought it and they wrapped it.

When Freddie and I went for tea, at Richloux, I gave him the present.

'What did you buy that for?' he asked.

'It's just a little present for you,' I said.

Once, Freddie was invited to the Lalique shop in Mount Street when Madame Lalique herself made a rare visit. She was the managing director of the company and had arrived in London to engrave her signature on a few pieces of her expensive lead crystal for favoured clients.

Freddie took Mary with him and returned with three beautiful clocks. His was signed 'To Freddie' and he had given one to Mary, which was also signed. Mine, which wasn't signed, was engraved with delicate irises running down both sides of the clock-face. Our two clocks took pride of place in his bedroom on either side of the bed.

When Mary gave birth to her baby son, Richard, in 1990, Freddie was thrilled. We visited mother and son in Queen Charlotte's Hospital many times and, when they went home, made many quick trips to Mary's flat to see how they were doing. We all gave Richard something special. Freddie arrived with armfuls of designer baby clothes bought during our trips to Switzerland as well as a small mountain of soft toys. I made a traditional wooden rocking cradle and then stencilled carousel horses and smiling clowns on the outside. To complete the cradle, Phoebe bought some beautiful linen bedding for it. Sadly the cradle was never used for Richard, but it was put to some good use – for storing the scores of cuddly toys.

Freddie was really delighted for Mary when Richard

came into the world. He loved holding him for a few minutes at a time but it was clear Freddie wasn't one of life's natural fathers; he liked children but from a safe distance.

9

PRUNING PALS

On a flying visit to Montreux in 1990, Freddie and I stayed at the Montreux Palace Hotel with Joe and Barbara Valentin. It was on that trip that he wrote his song 'Delilah', dedicated to his favourite cat.

The shops were still open when the four of us were walking back from the studio at the end of the day. Freddie was now on the look-out for beautiful linen, mostly tablecloths. Displayed in one shop window was something so camp we all burst out laughing. It was a Minnie and Mickey Mouse night outfit with shirt, shorts and a Wee Willie Winkie bobble hat. Barbara slipped back to buy it as a present for Freddie, which she gave him back at the hotel.

Later Joe and I turned in, but Freddie and Barbara didn't. They were in the mood to talk all night.

I got up at seven in the morning and went into the sitting room where Freddie and Barbara were still wide awake and going strong. He looked a sight. He was wearing his new Minnie and Mickey outfit, including the Wee Willie Winkie hat.

'Oh, it's that time already,' he said. 'Jim, I've written a new song. It's about my Delilah.'

He did sleep for a few hours that morning but, when he got up, he would spend his whole time tweaking his Delilah lyrics and trying out different lines on me. My favourite line was included in the final version: 'You make me slightly mad when you pee all over my Chippendale suite.'

For Joe's birthday in 1990 Freddie despatched me to New Convent Garden market, in south London, with £500 to buy as many different blooms in as many different colours as possible. I bought so many I filled the Volvo completely. When I got back to the house, Freddie was waiting. Joe was out and we spent the next two hours arranging all the flowers. We filled every vase and jug we could find. The house had never seen so many arrangements at one time and when Joe got back he was bowled over.

'Surprise!' Freddie said. 'Happy birthday!'

Later that night we all went out for a celebratory supper with the birthday boy. But Freddie and I didn't stay long as he said he was feeling too tired.

That same month Joe told everyone in Garden Lodge that he had some bad news. He, too, was not well.

'You mean you're HIV?' I asked.

'No,' he said. 'I've actually got full-blown Aids.'

What can you say? I'm sorry? Nothing of any use came into my mind. It would be another blow to contend with in Garden Lodge. We were all worried about what the press would make of it if they discovered that Joe was also ill. We had visions of the sick headlines and guessed our house would be dubbed 'Aids Lodge'. It all made us more determined than ever to pull together and stay optimistic.

Despite putting a brave face on things for everyone else's benefit at Garden Lodge, privately I began to get very anxious about my own health. I thought I could be HIV positive as well. The more I reluctantly thought about it, the more it seemed likely. So I decided to have an Aids test but to tell no one. I did it in total secrecy under a pseudonym. On the excuse of going to see a friend, I slipped out of Garden Lodge for a day and travelled to a hospital in Brighton.

Before the doctor would agree to take a blood sample for testing I had to undergo special counselling. The full implications of proving positive were explained honestly and compassionately. I told them I realised all the consequences and wanted to proceed.

That night back at Garden Lodge I found it impossible to sleep. I had told the hospital that I could handle the news if it was going to be bad. But I wasn't so sure in my own mind that I really could. What would I do?

A few days later I rang for the results.

'I'm very sorry, you're positive,' said the doctor. But I didn't have full-blown Aids.

I was dazed. I didn't tell Freddie. He had enough to cope with; my news could only upset him. I buried myself in work in the garden and workshop and put thoughts of my own future out of my mind. But the thought of it kept coming back to me each night as I struggled to sleep and stop my mind from racing.

Freddie and I went out to Syon Park one day and bought bedding plants for the garden. As Terry was loading the plants into the car, a photographer from the *Sun* who had been following us took a picture. It appeared the next day, with a story claiming, incorrectly, that it was the first time Freddie had been out of Garden Lodge for two months.

Whenever Freddie saw the television commercial for cat-food featuring snowy-coated Arthur he said how much he'd like a white cat. Then he dismissed the idea because he thought it would be impossible to keep such a cat clean.

I went to the pet shop in Kensington High Street one morning and in the window there were five kittens from the same litter. Each was completely white save for a few marks which were hardly noticeable.

It was as much as I could do to stop myself buying one there and then for Freddie.

I went back to Garden Lodge, put on my waders and started cleaning out the isolation tank for the koi. Joe and Phoebe came through the back door.

'We've got a favour to ask you,' said Joe.

'Oh yes?' I replied.

'I've just come from Kensington High Street and ...' he began.

'And you passed the pet shop and saw the kittens?' I said.

'Yes,' he said. 'They're only £25 each. Phoebe and I will give you the money. Will you get the whitest one for Freddie?'

'Why don't you buy it?' I asked.

'We decided to ask you,' Joe said, 'because if you buy it then Freddie won't scream and shout if he's annoyed.'

'I'll go,' I said. 'But only on one condition: that if Freddie does start screaming and shouting, you'll share the blame.'

So I set off for the shop at once and hoped to get back to the house before Freddie got out of bed.

I drove to the shop in the Volvo. There were only three kittens left. I picked one out, drove back to Garden Lodge and slipped the kitten into my jacket as I walked in. Freddie was in the garden, so I walked slowly towards him, beaming. Freddie scowled at me.

'You bastard!' he said. 'You've got another cat, haven't you?'

'How did you know?' I asked.

'His tail is sticking out from under your jacket!' he said. I took the kitten from my jacket and put her on the ground. Freddie bent down, stroked her and couldn't resist picking her up. Freddie quickly christened our sixth cat. 'We'll call her Lily!' he said. So Lily it was.

Although he adored the new kitten, he wondered whether her arrival would upset the other five cats. Oscar was a cat who preferred his own company, and the arrival of the latest kitten proved to be the final straw. Increasingly he would roam off to visit other homes in the area and adopted one neighbour especially. He even started sleeping out at night, but Freddie didn't mind.

'If Oscar's happy, then that's all that matters,' he would say.

Freddie's health continued to deteriorate. He was now very thin and found it difficult to sleep, so I decided to move to my own room permanently. Some nights I would still sleep with him, but usually I just lay next to him on top of the bedclothes. He'd snuggle up next to me for comfort. Freddie nicknamed my new bedroom the Ice Box as I slept with the window wide open, even in the middle of winter.

One Sunday he got up and went downstairs to discover I hadn't got out of bed. I had the flu. He came to see me, got into bed with me and cuddled up. He kissed me.

'Oh, you poor thing,' he said.

He certainly didn't seem worried about catching flu from me. We were all conscious of his need to avoid any infection and especially colds and flu as they might prove fatal, but that day he didn't worry about himself at all. He didn't catch the flu from me and remained resilient.

It was while he was nursing me through my flu that Freddie decided it was time he did something about my room. He settled on the idea of commissioning contemporary Biedermeier-style furniture to be made for me by a company in Chelsea. He would design a coffee table, then a bed surround, himself. He flicked through books on Biedermeier to get ideas and started outlining his thoughts for the coffee table on a sketch pad. It looked wonderful. It was round and two-tiered. The legs were round ebonised wood balls decorated with little gold stars. The bed surround looked great, but Freddie felt it needed a few of his finishing touches. He returned with his bag of ormolu fittings and found a few large ones to decorate it. Freddie also bought me a new looking glass and three antique Biedermeier chests of drawers. A few weeks later he reserved more pieces of furniture from the supplier.

When he sent Terry to pay and collect them he proved he'd learnt at least something from me.

'Don't forget to ask for a discount!' he said.

When I moved into my own room permanently I left all the pictures on my side of Freddie's bed because I didn't want him to feel that I had moved out for good. The only thing I took with me was a little Cartier alarm clock. As time went on, Freddie started moving some of the photographs into my room one by one.

That move into the Pink Room also marked the point from which almost all normal sexual relations ended between us. It was clear that sex was no longer a pleasure for him but an exhausting ordeal instead. So we settled for the next best thing: gentle kissing and heart-felt cuddles. Those cuddling sessions would be as rewarding in their way as any sex we ever had.

Freddie's medication for Aids took a new turn when he was fitted with a small catheter on his chest below his left shoulder. It had a small rubber stopper and the whole thing was so small it was barely noticeable. It certainly never interfered when we cuddled up to each other. The catheter made it simpler for Freddie to be given medicine intravenously. More importantly, it allowed him to keep on the go. By slipping the medication in his pocket and hiding the tube leading to the catheter, he could walk around and even go out.

Previously I had helped Joe and Phoebe give Freddie some of his medication. He had to take a white powder mixed with water, so I'd fix those for him or get out his pills. But once he went on to intravenous medication and had the catheter fitted, everything became much more complicated.

It was suggested that I might like to help administer the medicine intravenously, but I asked to be excused. I didn't want to take on the responsibility. And there was also a risk of infection. My job entailed working outside, often up to my arms in muck in the flower beds or up to my waist in filthy water in the koi pool. The garden was a breeding ground for all kinds of germs. If I was to give Freddie his medication every few hours, I would have to be forever scrubbing up. Even Joe, clean as he was since he was working in the kitchen all day long, spent half an hour each time sterilising his hands and arms. I was worried that I might not scrub up thoroughly enough. It was an unnecessary risk.

Freddie understood entirely and didn't seem at all put out by my decision.

As Freddie's health continued to deteriorate, I used to have a quiet word with Mary. I reassured her time and again that I would always be there for her. If there was ever anything she needed she had only to ask.

In the summer, quite out of the blue, Freddie increased my wages from £600 to £1000 per month. Sadly, my wage rise was the reason for an argument between Freddie and Mary.

The accountants were on holiday, so Freddie had to sign the monthly pay cheques. I had never questioned how much I was paid. I knew that Joe and Phoebe were paid more, but they were on duty twenty-four hours a day. I never wanted to know exactly what they were paid; it was none of my business. I was just the boyfriend. I was happy with my lot. I would have tended Freddie's garden whether or not I was paid. I loved to watch the simple pleasure it gave him.

The day Freddie signed the cheques, I was in the koi pool in my waders. He called me into the house and I went to the front door where I tried to kick off the waders.

'Oh, leave the bloody things on,' he said. 'Come on over here. I want you to give me a big cuddle. I've got some news for you.'

So, still in my waders, I walked over to him and we hugged.

He said: 'You won't get it this month, but you'll get it next. You're getting a pay rise.'

Then Freddie said something which would prove very important to me in the months ahead. It was always understood that ownership of the house once he had died would technically pass to Mary. However, he said he hoped I would stay living there as long as I liked and reiterated that it was my home as much as his. He added that, if I wanted to move out, he had made Mary promise that I could have whatever I wanted from Garden Lodge.

I was very relieved, but I didn't like talking about such things so coldly.

'I don't want to hear about you dying,' I said. 'And if you want those wishes carried out, write them down.'

During the year Freddie gave me several things for our retreat in Ireland, which was now finished and ready for decorating. Furniture deemed to be surplus to requirements was stored in the attic at Garden Lodge.

'If there's anything you want for our home in Ireland, then help yourself,' he said. Then he came with me to look. Among other things, we sent back to Ireland his old double bed from Stafford Terrace and two Victorian bedside tables.

Freddie kept many possessions he didn't have space for in storage. So he decided that summer that it was time to get everything back to Garden Lodge to share out among the family.

When the storage chests arrived at Garden Lodge I was away in Ireland for a few days. They had been spread out on the lawn and Freddie dived into them, deciding who should get what. Joe, Phoebe, Mary and the two maids shared most of the contents, mostly knick-knacks and old designer clothes.

When I got home Freddie told me some of the things he'd come across.

'I haven't left you out,' he said. 'There's another trunk which no one has touched. That's yours.'

When I later opened up the trunk there were hats and ornaments. Then I found the original lyrics for his most famous song: 'Bohemian Rhapsody'. They were handwritten by Freddie on a sheet of A4 lined paper. I left everything in the trunk, including the lyrics, and stored it in the workshop for safe-keeping.

I was in the workshop one afternoon trying to mend an antique silver photograph frame treasured by Freddie's parents when I had an accident with an electric plane. I took a chunk out of my finger and there was blood everywhere. I made for the kitchen where I found Phoebe and Joe. Joe was always squeamish at the sight of blood.

'Have you got any big plasters, Joe?' I said.

'What have you done?' Joe asked.

When I showed him my finger he gulped. This would need more than a sticking plaster.

'You'd better go to hospital to have that stitched,' he said.

I dismissed it as a scratch and Freddie came in.

'What's all the noise about?' he asked.

Joe said: 'Jim has cut himself badly but doesn't want to go to the hospital.'

Freddie looked at the wound and agreed with Joe and Phoebe that it needed hospital treatment. When I said it was a fuss over nothing he got annoyed.

'All right, please yourself then,' he said. But to save argument I went to the hospital, and ended up having two stitches. It was much more serious than I had thought.

In the end I did finally fix the frame for Freddie's parents. Around that time I was making another of my tables as a present from Freddie and me to chauffeur Graham Hamilton and his friend Gordon. So Freddie blamed them for my accident!

That summer Freddie and I nearly parted company after a nasty argument about nothing. For some reason I upset Freddie and we had a fight. These things would usually blow over in a day or so, but this time it dragged on for days.

I went to work, as usual, in the garden and during the morning Mary and Freddie came out into the garden and sat talking near the pool. Later, when I went back in the house, the air was decidedly frosty. Freddie kept his distance.

The next day things were no better. I was in the garden and Joe, looking most uncomfortable, told me the news.

'Freddie thinks it would be a good idea if you left,' he said.

I was flabbergasted. I still didn't know exactly how we had come to fall out, but Freddie had the drawbridge up and the portcullis firmly down.

'Fine,' I said. I sounded calm but I was really quite distraught. 'If that's the way he feels, well, OK,' I said. 'But I need time to find myself a place to live.'

The next day I got another message, this time from Mary, that when I'd found myself alternative accommodation I would still be welcome to work six days a week as the gardener at Garden Lodge. She told me I could not have the use of the Volvo Freddie had given me for my birthday. I'd be permitted only an hour for lunch and my hours would be 9am – 6pm.

The only thing I could think about was whether I could afford somewhere to live, so I said: 'When I find my own place, I want my wages reviewed. Gardeners in central London are getting an average of £12.50 an hour.' I was on about £3.

I found myself a flat, a short six-month lease in Hammersmith Grove, which had been advertised in *Loot* with the unusual tag 'To share with Sir Charles' – a cat. The owners needed references, so I asked Mary whether she would mind speaking for me. That afternoon I was in the conservatory and got word from my new landlord that my references were fine and that I could move in immediately.

Freddie came up to me.

'You don't want to go, do you?' he said. 'I don't want you to go.'

'But I was under the impression you *did* want me to go,' I said. I was puzzled.

'I was just angry over something,' he said. As we talked it over it became clear that even he didn't remember how the argument had started and nor did anyone else. What I was so sad about was how my friends at Garden Lodge had seemed quite happy to see me go.

That night in the bedroom, lying next to Freddie, I asked him about the others. 'Well, whose advice did you take?' I said. 'I know they've all been giving you advice over the last few days. Who did you listen to?' I was determined to find out who it was who had been making trouble for me at Garden Lodge.

'I took my own advice,' he said and he wrinkled his face as if to say 'subject closed'. I asked him why he'd let it get so out of control, but he wouldn't answer. He asked me to forget the whole thing. It wasn't easy. I was extremely hurt and depressed by what had happened. I couldn't imagine who would get him so worked up over nothing.

Elton John and Freddie had fallen out with each other years ago, but by *Live Aid* they were back on good speaking terms. That summer Elton started coming to the house and he became one of Freddie's few regular, trusted visitors until the very end.

The first time Elton came for Sunday lunch was a day to remember. As we were laying the table Joe told me I was sitting at the end of the table with Freddie on my left and Elton on my right.

'So don't put salt on your food!' he said.

'Why ever not?' I asked.

'You'll see, Elton will do it for you!' he said.

Elton wore a tracksuit and baseball cap, which stayed on his head for the entire visit. He was fairly rotund then, but on a strict diet. He didn't have any meat, just vegetables. Nor would he drink anything but water. When we started eating I soon discovered what Joe had meant. Elton liked his seasoning and he shook the salt so vigorously over his plate that he saved me the trouble of putting it on mine.

In the autumn Freddie told Joe his right leg was playing him up. This was the same leg that had the painful open wound at the side of the calf. It had always been troublesome to him. Before we met he'd broken the same leg larking around in a Munich gay club. Joe went weight-training and suggested some exercises for Freddie to try. I turned on my heel and went off to order Freddie a top-of-the-range exercise cycle. When the bike arrived two weeks later Freddie was still having problems with his leg. Freddie loved it at first, but sessions on it were to be no more than a passing fad. Joe and I struggled to carry it to the minstrels' gallery, and from time to time Freddie would do five or ten minutes on it under Joe's supervision.

Freddie's birthday in September 1990 was a lavish, dressy

affair, an *haute cuisine* dinner party held at Garden Lodge. It was attended by some twenty guests, mostly couples. Mary was there with Piers, Dr Gordon Atkinson with his friend Roger, chauffeurs Graham Hamilton and Gordon, Jim Beach and his wife Claudia, Terry and his wife Sharon, Mike and Linda Moran, record engineer Dave Richards with his wife Colette, Dave Clark, Trevor Clarke, Barbara Valentin, Peter Straker, Joe and his friends Tony Evans, Phoebe and me.

This night was to be the last year Freddie celebrated his birthday with any kind of bang. To ensure it was a night that everyone would remember, Freddie gave each of us a memento of the occasion from Tiffany and Co, a present left on each place setting.

When Freddie penned the song 'I'm Going Slightly Mad' it was after another through-the-night session with Peter Straker. Freddie explained he had the phrase 'I'm Going Slightly Mad' on his brain and told Peter what sort of thing he wanted to say in the song. The inspiration for it was the master of camp one-liners, Noël Coward.

Freddie set about with Peter trying to come up with a succession of goofy lyrics, each funnier than the last. He screamed when they came up with things like 'I'm knitting with only one needle' and 'I'm driving on only three wheels these days'. But the master-stroke was: 'I think I'm a banana tree'. Once that came out there was no stopping Freddie and Straker – they were then in full flow. I went to bed to fall asleep listening to their laughter wafting upstairs.

It was while I was away in Ireland for a few days that Freddie and Peter Straker fell out and the rift was never to be mended. Peter was noticeable by his absence, particularly at weekends when before he would invariably come round for a drink or a meal. I asked Freddie why we hadn't seen anything of him.

'He upset me at Joe's Café one day,' he said, but refused to say what had happened. So I asked Joe and Phoebe.

Apparently, Freddie had arranged to meet Peter for lunch at Joe's Café in Knightsbridge. When he arrived, a little late, he appeared to be drunk. The restaurant wasn't a regular haunt of Freddie's and he felt that Peter had shown him up in public. Freddie decided he didn't want to be associated with him again.

But looking back on it, Peter shouldn't feel too awful about what happened. Freddie's behaviour at the time was increasingly guided by his failing health. He may even have been a little jealous of Peter, who could still treat life as one long party just as Freddie had once done. It wasn't only Peter who got the cold shoulder at that time. Barbara Valentin also drifted out of sight, as did Graham Hamilton and Gordon.

Relations cooled between Freddie and Gordon because Gordon couldn't hold his tongue. Freddie expected total loyalty and discretion from those around him. When Graham or Gordon drove Freddie, they'd drop the names of the other VIPs they had had in the back of their car. Freddie believed that they must also talk freely to their other passengers about him.

The final straw came when I went out for a drink one night to Champions, a gay pub in Notting Hill Gate. Gordon was in the pub and came over to say hello, introducing me to a young friend drinking with him. A little later I left and walked to the nearby Gate Club, a gay club.

After I'd been there about half an hour, the young man Gordon had introduced me to arrived and made a beeline for me.

'I know everything about you,' he said. 'I know you're Freddie Mercury's boyfriend.' He went on to tell me bits and pieces of gossip he'd learnt from Gordon.

I was speechless. He was a total stranger and he knew some very private things about us.

'Who told you all this?' I asked, though the answer was obvious. I left the club at once and got home about midnight. Freddie was wide awake in bed.

'You look livid. What's wrong?' he asked. I told him what had happened and he shook his head.

'Right,' he said. And we didn't see much of Graham and Gordon after that.

In November Queen signed a new multi-million-pound record deal which Jim Beach had negotiated in America with Hollywood Records, owned by the giant Walt Disney Corporation. It placed the band in the enviable position of having Disney's finest animators, using state-of-the-art techniques, at their disposal to help make their videos.

The same month Freddie tried to ban the *Sun* from Garden Lodge after the headline 'It's Official! Freddie Is Seriously Ill' appeared. The paper reported Brian May's remarks that Freddie was sick. 'I never want to see the *Sun* in here again,' he said. But the ban didn't last. I was the one who bought the newspapers and flicked through them to take out anything I thought would upset Freddie. I'd tell him the newsagent had run out of that particular paper and leave it at that.

The staff party for everyone at the Queen office in 1990 turned out to be the last. The band never showed the staff their videos ahead of their release, but this year they made an exception and showed the extraordinary 'Innuendo' video, which had been made with all the latest Disney animation techniques.

The video was the creation of the Torpedo Twins, Rudy and Hans, and the animation had been painstaking and slow. The results were remarkable. It was later deemed too controversial for America, because this was the time of the Gulf War and the record company was sensitive about the song's pacifist theme. Every day new edits of the video would keep arriving for Freddie to view. Eventually it was re-edited, omitting letters from words in the Koran, the sacred book of Islam.

For Christmas I bought Freddie some antique coloured glass goblets, but I almost blew the surprise. In a shop window I spotted six black glasses with clear stems which, when I took a closer look, turned out to be a deep red colour. When I got them back to Garden Lodge I bumped into Freddie. He asked why I looked so pleased with myself and I stupidly showed him. 'This is your Christmas present. Have a look,' I said. Then I put them away in a cupboard.

Around noon on Christmas Eve I set off to buy myself a pair of denim jeans in Earl's Court. I felt furious with myself for having shown Freddie his present. As I passed the little antique shop, the owner was just unlocking and noticed me.

'Those glasses you bought,' he said.

'Yes?' I answered.

'I meant to say when you bought them, I've got another half dozen inside,' he said. 'They're part of a set of twelve.'

'How much?' I asked. He offered a slight discount, and I bought them. I raced back to Garden Lodge, kept well away from Freddie, wrapped them up and placed them under the tree.

On Christmas morning I woke up with excruciating tooth-ache. It was so bad I had to find an emergency dentist and he took my tooth out.

Like me, Freddie loathed dentists. He went for a check-up once a year. He was in both agony and ecstasy when being worked on by the hygienist, because he loved her aggressiveness when she was on the job. He would come out afterwards and say: 'She really gets at them!'

Freddie's teeth protruded because other teeth had grown behind his front ones. They should have been taken out when he was a child, but it hadn't happened. After he became successful he said he'd have them fixed, but the truth is he wasn't vain enough to bother about them. And he knew his teeth were his trademark – the one thing that caricatures of him always made a point of.

Although his teeth were so prominent, I think he had a lovely smile. He became self-conscious and embarrassed only when he was having a really hearty laugh – when he guffawed like a donkey and showed all his teeth off. Then his hand would fly to hide the lower part of his face.

After Christmas lunch we went to open our presents. I took my present for Freddie from underneath the tree and handed it to him. As he tore the paper off and spied the dark red goblets beneath, he looked up at me.

'These are in the cupboard!' he said.

'No, they're not,' I told him. 'These are another six.'

They were given pride of place in a display cabinet.

Freddie was now beginning to become very frail, but 1991 started terrifically for him in musical terms. The release of the single 'Innuendo' in the middle of January took him and Queen right back to the place they deserved, the top of the charts. The album came out in February and also shot straight to the top.

On Valentine's Day Freddie was out of the house recording the video to 'I'm Going Slightly Mad', which would be their next single release. But that didn't stop Freddie playing a joke on me. The cats and I had Garden Lodge to ourselves, as Phoebe was out and Joe and Terry were with Freddie at the shoot. The phone rang. It was Terry, asking if Phoebe had 'got what Freddie wanted'. Just then Phoebe came in and I passed the phone across. Freddie came on the line and I heard Phoebe tell him: 'I've only got one of them.'

When Freddie got home, at about 8pm, I was sitting in an armchair alone in the lounge, with the hallway door closed. When he arrived there were whispers in the hall, then a flurry of activity. He came in carrying a large package wrapped in brown paper.

'Surprise!' he said, handing me the large, heavy, oblong shape.

'What is it?' I asked.

'It's a surprise!' said Freddie, bright-eyed. I then unwrapped a beautiful gilt-framed Victorian oil painting that I'd noticed a day or so earlier in a Sotheby's auction catalogue. Its subject was two small kittens playing with a snail on a garden path and it was titled *Surprise*.

'I know exactly where we're going to put it, as well,' added Freddie.

'Where?' I asked.

'You can shift that picture there,' he said, pointing to a part of the wall which could be seen from all angles. It stayed there for a while, but Freddie had really bought it with the Irish retreat in mind.

Freddie also bought a second picture. It was massive, and the only picture of a man that he bought. It was of a young boy looking radiant and strong as he stood on life's threshold. It was sent off immediately for essential restoration work, and we didn't see it for some months.

Freddie was very weak for the filming of the video for 'I'm Going Slightly Mad'. He had to be caked in make-up and wore a thick black wig.

Because he looked so different, when I turned up one day to take a look I didn't recognise him. There were also some penguins there for the shoot and in quiet moments Freddie took himself off to be with them and give them water. Under studio lights they were baking and, ill as he was, he was only concerned for their welfare.

'It's far too hot for them,' he complained. It was really a distraction to keep his mind off his own problems.

Freddie decided he wanted to buy a place in Montreux. He took some of us to the Duck House for a holiday – including Mary and baby Richard and Terry and his family. One day we all went off to look at a serene fifties' chalet-style lake-house with its own moorings and, what I fancied, a garden. But it wasn't suitable; because of the security we really needed a flat. And we wouldn't be living there for most of the time.

Then Jim Beach found a three-bedroomed penthouse flat in an exquisite building called La Tourelle. We flew over to see it. It was parquet-floored throughout with a spacious sitting room, large windows and a balcony looking across the lake and city. There was also a second, smaller, cosier sitting room, and at the back a kitchen and three bedrooms – for Joe, Freddie and me.

When I got back to London I received an urgent phone call from my sister Patricia. She said that for months the *Daily Mirror* had been trying to track down the location of our Irish hideaway. They had offered £1000 to the man who had transported several pieces of furniture over for us to give them the address. The paper was under the impression that they had a hot exclusive: Freddie Mercury had secretly moved to Ireland to hide from the world. Instead they settled for 'revealing' to my family that I was gay. My family already knew and couldn't care less. The press were quickly sent packing.

One time when I got home from another flying visit to Ireland I sat in the kitchen with Freddie, showing him the latest photographs of the bungalow's progress. It was turning out to be monstrous, the kind of thing Prince Charles might call a carbuncle. But Freddie was pleased with the way it looked, and he said how much he would like to see it for himself.

'Well, why don't you?' I said. 'We can get an early morning flight out of Heathrow. We'll be in Dublin by ten and it'll take another couple of hours.'

'Will I have to meet all your family?' he asked.

That's how shy he was.

'No, you won't have to meet the family,' I told him. 'The only one you might meet is my mother.'

Freddie knew that that wouldn't be a problem. He thought for a moment and got very interested in the idea. He suggested that perhaps we could hire a helicopter to get us there even more quickly, and I made some enquiries.

But a few days later Freddie's enthusiasm fizzled out. Ireland was unknown territory to him and he would find that hard going. And his illness was making him weaker and more tired than he was letting on. He wasn't strong enough for a six-hour round trip anywhere. It was enough just to find the will to carry on.

He never did set foot in the bungalow, but it feels like he's been there. He followed its progress so closely at all stages that I see and feel him in every room.

Around April 1991 Joe became depressed about his Aids. He poured out his heart to Freddie, and said that he worried that when Freddie died he wouldn't have a home any more. Freddie's compassion kicked in at once.

'Well,' he said. 'You find a house and I'll buy it for you.'

A few weeks later Joe found a small house in Chiswick which Freddie bought for him.

10

LETTING GO

In May 1991 Queen released their single 'Headlong'. The lyrics seemed to sum up what was facing us at Garden Lodge: 'You're rushing headlong out of control, and you think you're so strong. But there ain't no stopping, and there's nothing you can do about it at all.' There was certainly no way of reversing Freddie's weakening condition and we all knew it. But he was cheered greatly by his new flat in Switzerland. We went over to Montreux a couple of times to see it. Freddie knew exactly how he wanted the flat decorated and chose everything himself. The only thing that Joe and I were allowed to choose was the colour of our bedrooms – pastel green and pastel blue respectively. On the first visit Freddie wanted an instant garden created on the balconies, so I was sent off to blow a small fortune on plants.

'I want plenty of everything and lots of greenery,' said Freddie.

Three hours later the balconies were transformed, and complemented the extraordinary views out across the lake.

Freddie hired Montreux's most exclusive interior designers, demanding vehemently that the whole thing must be finished by Christmas which he'd decided to spend quietly there.

The last picture Freddie bought was a fabulous Tissot from Christie's. It was a portrait of the artist's mistress, Kathleen

Newton, in a bonnet with her left hand delicately raised to her cheek. Freddie paid £160,000 for it. But there was a sad side to the picture, and it was deeply ironic. Kathleen Newton looked fit and well in the picture, but in fact she was suffering from a terminal illness. She died young a short time after the picture was painted.

That summer Freddie posed for a camera for the very last time – mine. It happened like this. I was out in the garden photographing some of the flowers in full bloom and Freddie walked towards me. I trained the lens on him and he told me to hold on – he wanted to move back a bit so it wasn't a close-up. Then he posed while I took four pictures, and he managed a smile for each. He was so pale and drawn that he knew he didn't look his best, but it didn't matter a bit; of all the pictures I have of Freddie, those are the ones I love most.

In August we heard that Paul Prenter had died from Aids. Freddie was visibly shaken. Freddie knew Paul had the disease but I don't think he realised how quickly it might claim his life. Paul's death troubled him for many weeks, and inevitably reminded him of his own fate.

The same month I asked Freddie what he wanted for his birthday. 'Some lovely Irish crystal champagne glasses for the flat in Switzerland,' he said. So, on the way home from a visit to Ireland, that's what I bought and, unlike the previous year, this time I kept them a complete secret. For most of the next few weeks I hid myself in my workshop, making a presentation box in wood to keep the new glasses in. I French polished it, then lined it with blue velvet.

Freddie's birthday, 5 September 1991, was a very quiet affair. He came downstairs in the morning in his dressing gown for a cup of tea. 'My God,' I thought to myself. He seemed to look so frail that day.

With us in the kitchen were Mary and Dave Clark, who'd both come by to wish him a happy birthday. The box I was giving Freddie was hidden from him in a kitchen cupboard and, after Mary and Dave had given him their presents, I thought it was time for mine, too.

'Well,' I said to Freddie, taking the box from the cupboard, 'happy birthday.' He looked at the box and ran his hands over it, saying how beautiful it was. A few minutes later it dawned on me that Freddie thought the gift was the box itself, and he seemed happy enough with that.

'Aren't you going to open it, then?' asked Dave, who knew the glasses were inside. When Freddie did, he looked so surprised. 'Well, you did say you'd like some lovely champagne glasses for the flat in Montreux,' I said. Sadly, the glasses never did get to Switzerland.

Freddie's forty-fifth birthday was perhaps the quietest of his life. He was very aware that he wasn't on top form and that he could no longer disguise the fact that he was coming to the end of his life. He didn't want a huge bash for his friends because he didn't want them to see how sad he looked. The only thing he wanted from anyone for his last birthday was privacy.

Yet the press were still on his tail. One day we went for lunch to Pontevecchio's in Earl's Court. The manager told us that a *News of the World* reporter and photographer were hanging around outside, waiting for Freddie to emerge. Liam Byrne, the manager of the Coleherne pub nearby, had phoned to tip us off. So Freddie and I made our exit by the back door.

In October the band released their single 'The Show Must Go On', with the B-side 'Keep Yourself Alive'. As Freddie expected, the press weren't slow to report its questioning, haunting lyrics. They speculated on possible hidden meanings in lyrics like 'What are we living for?' and 'I'll soon be turning round the corner now' at a time when he looked so frail. To me, the most autobiographical line was: 'My make-up may be flaking but my smile still stays on.' That was true. No matter how ill Freddie felt, he never grumbled to anyone or sought sympathy of any kind. It was his battle, no one else's, and he always wore a brave face against the ever-increasing odds against him.

The last video Freddie made was for the single 'These Are the Days of Our Lives'. (It was released, shortly after his death, on the flip-side of 'Bohemian Rhapsody'.) It seemed a very apt swansong. When Freddie was making the video he looked worse than I had ever seen him. Now the thick make-up he used to disguise the markings on his face only seemed to highlight his gaunt features. The security at the studio was very tight and only the essential technicians were there. During the shoot, Diana Moseley and I sat on the edge of the stage at Freddie's feet. At the end of the final take, Freddie gave a cheeky little grin and winked at me. I turned crimson, prompting Diana to say: 'For goodness sake, Jim, pull yourself together.'

Freddie was now very feeble, but he did summon up the strength to host one last special dinner party at Garden Lodge. It was to thank all the doctors who had nursed him through his illness. Dr Gordon Atkinson was there along with five other specialists, including a man called Dr Graham Moyle.

No one around that table knew of my condition, although I feel some may have had their suspicions. During the meal, Dr Moyle got around to the subject of my taking an Aids test. He didn't beat around the bush.

'Have the test,' he said. 'If you turn out to be HIV positive at least you'll know. And if you test negative you'll lose nothing more than a few grey hairs.'

I knew the answer anyway. A second opinion was likely to do nothing more than reinforce the sad truth. Still, taking a second test seemed a good idea, so I agreed.

Freddie wanted to visit the flat in Switzerland one last time. We flew there in a private jet: the two of us, Joe, Terry and Freddie's long-standing friend Tony King, who was Mick Jagger's assistant.

I went to see Dr Atkinson at his surgery to let him take a blood sample for the Aids test. As it would take a while to get the results back from the lab, he promised he would phone me in Montreux the moment he got them.

It was our third visit to the flat in Montreux, and it was clear that Freddie and I wouldn't be there together for a fourth and our planned quiet Christmas. We went out to restaurants every night for ten days, but now Freddie was very slow and needed a helping hand to walk.

He used the Swiss trip to find some peace in which to make a few final decisions. It was during that visit that he made the important decision to come off his medication and die. He decided not to let any of us know what he was doing. The fight against his disease was over; he was ready to slip away without any further struggle.

During our time at the flat Freddie began spending more time in his bedroom, retreating to his bed in T-shirt and boxer shorts to doze for large parts of the day. We took it in turns to look after him. Tony King stayed with Freddie the whole day, and Joe and I would leave Freddie to sleep when he felt too weak to chat.

Four days before we were due to return to London, Dr Atkinson was due to phone with the results of my Aids test. Although I knew what the result would be, I was a bundle of nerves. It was a one-in-a-million chance that the result of the first test had been a mistake. Freddie and Joe didn't know I was expecting a call that morning. Joe was around and I couldn't sit next to Freddie lying on the sofa watching television; I couldn't relax.

I paced the room for hours waiting for the call. I kept wondering how Freddie would take the news if I decided to come clean about my own condition. After I had almost worn the carpet bare from walking around in circles, Freddie asked me what was the matter.

'I'm bloody annoyed with our doctor,' I said. 'He promised me he'd phone with the results of the Aids test today.'

'Why don't you phone him yourself?' Freddie said.

I did. I got through and the doctor was very matter of fact about it all.

'I'm sorry, darling,' he said, 'you're HIV positive.'

I rang off and looked at Freddie.

'Well, what's the result?' he said.

'I'm positive,' I replied.

The colour drained from his face.

'The bastards,' he said, referring to whoever had given it to him, and whoever had given it to that person, and so on along the endless chain.

Later in the day, while Freddie was resting, Joe and I talked about my condition. He said he and Freddie knew what the result would be before I'd even made the call; I was pale and the outcome was written all over my face.

I became very depressed by it all. Regardless of my fate, I finally came to accept that Freddie wasn't going to live much longer. We were in the last few days before the end.

Most of the time I simply wanted to cry. While Freddie was asleep, I would go for a short walk or sit alone chain-smoking. I'd walk through the night rather than go to bed, as I knew I wouldn't sleep. One time Tony joined me in a long, slow walk around the lake. We got chatting.

He told me of some of the things he and Freddie had been discussing. With me in mind, Tony asked Freddie: 'What's going to happen to the boys?'

'Well, Jim will be staying in Garden Lodge,' Freddie replied.

Tony, astonished, told him: 'But Mary doesn't get on with Jim.'

According to Tony that night, Freddie answered: 'Well, they'll just have to work it out, won't they?' I wasn't surprised to hear that Mary didn't like me.

A few days later Freddie and I were together on the sofa in the lounge watching an old thirties' black-and-white movie. The heroine asked her partner: 'Will we spend the rest of our lives together?' Freddie looked at me and asked the same thing.

'Of course we will,' I answered. 'Don't be silly.'

A lump came into my throat.

Coming back from Switzerland, Freddie was in good spirits. We'd arranged for him to be sped through customs. In his final few weeks he'd refer to it proudly. 'Even Liz Taylor doesn't get away with that, dear!' he'd say.

Of course, Freddie was given special permission to avoid the queues at customs and passport control because he was so ill. He tired easily and looked terrible, and it would have been cruel to allow him to attract the attentions of the crowd. None of us were allowed to accompany Freddie and for a while he was split from the rest of us, dependent on total strangers for the first time in years. We tried protesting, but it was no use. We still had to go through immigration like everyone else while poor frail Freddie was left in the Customs Hall to wait for us.

'It would have been just as easy for me to have come through with you lot,' he laughed. But he said that he had been well looked after by the customs staff.

Back at Garden Lodge, Freddie set out on the last three weeks of his life. As in Switzerland, he remained in good spirits, though he took to his bed for long parts of the day. He didn't once talk about work. Some days he'd get up in the morning and come down in his dressing gown for a cup of tea before returning to his room for the rest of the day. And I'd take him a cup of tea, along with his beloved Delilah for company.

We kept ourselves sane by doing jobs around the house and still pretending that everything was normal. I got round to putting fairy lights in the second magnolia tree by the corner of the house. It made the place look like a fairy grotto, but who cared so long as it made Freddie a little happier.

I waited until Freddie and I were alone in the bedroom before showing him the lights.

'You haven't passed any remark about the tree,' I said.

'What tree?' he asked.

'Come over to the window and I'll show you,' I said.

He walked to the window and his face lit up when he saw the tree twinkling away.

'Oh, you've done it,' he said and hugged me.

Before, he would have responded differently, perhaps snapping sarcastically: 'Why has it taken you so long?' But now he no longer had the strength.

I found solace in working in the garden. I lived for the enjoyment he could get from looking at me and the garden from his window. Right up to the very last day I worked on the garden. Even on the Sunday he died, I mowed the lawn.

I abandoned a planned trip to Ireland as time was so clearly running out for Freddie. Joe told me it was in that second week that Freddie came off most of his medication except painkillers. It was a decision he took against the advice of his doctors.

Much of the time Freddie slept or watched television. Joe or Phoebe stayed with him through the day, relieved for short breaks by Mary or Dave Clark. Dave came every day, and we appreciated his help immensely.

Although I was busy working in the garden where he could see me, Freddie needed to hear from me more and more that I loved him. So I got into the habit of flying upstairs and quickly sticking my head around the door.

'Hey,' I'd say. 'I love you!'

Then I'd run back down to get on with the gardening. I knew it made him feel good for a few minutes at least. Sometimes when I got downstairs again I'd look up at his window and he'd be there waiting for me to emerge outside; then he'd blow me a kiss.

I spent the evenings alone with Freddie. We would talk or watch television, or I would doze alongside him. He'd rest his frail head in the cradle of my arm and I'd gently massage his scalp.

Joe, Phoebe and I also started taking turns to stay with Freddie through the night, usually lying awake next to him on constant stand-by. We had an intercom system installed so we could summon one another, and pagers so we could be reached instantly. We wanted to be with him at the end.

In the last ten days before Freddie died, the press set up camp outside Garden Lodge. In the early morning one or two would arrive, followed by more as the day went on. After an hour or so there'd be six or seven dozen.

One of the reporters was a grey-haired man with a big moustache who slipped me a note for Freddie. Letters from the press were given to us daily and this man's was typical. He said he and his colleagues were dreadfully sorry for causing a nuisance, but if Freddie could come out to have just one photograph taken they could quash the 'terrible rumours'.

A few days later pushier reporters and photographers began covering both entrances to Garden Lodge. They got up to everything. They'd stand on the walls on the other side of the road to snatch pictures of the house. Their lenses were trained on all the windows. Anyone arriving or leaving the house was instantly interrogated and they ran after visitors down the street. I usually kept my head well down, said nothing and barked at them: 'I suppose you'll want to know what colour toilet paper I use next?' When they asked how Freddie was, I'd say he wasn't at Garden Lodge but out of the country.

I got my own back one day, too. A favourite place for the press to wait was sitting on the other side of the wall to a sunshed we nicknamed the 'Number 27 bus shelter'. I got the water pressure machine from the garage and turned it on, training the spray over the roof. There were a number of startled screams from the other side of the wall. I had soaked them.

Terry came in for more than his fair share of flak from the press. They knew he was one of Freddie's most trusted employees and towards the end he too got his own back.

We were stopped on the way in to Garden Lodge the day the body of rogue newspaper proprietor Robert Maxwell, who owned the *Daily Mirror*, was found washed up in the Canary Islands.

'How's Freddie doing today, then?' asked the *Mirror* reporter.

'Better than Maxwell!' said Terry.

One night Roger Taylor was pulling out of The Mews late at night and made a sharp left turn into Logan Place. The photographers let off their flashes and, blinded for a moment, he crashed into a police car.

The siege of Garden Lodge posed enormous problems for some of the celebrities who came to pay their last respects. We used a secret entrance in and out of the premises, via the garage adjoined to The Mews, to let them slip in and out. Elton John would warn us by car telephone that he was on his way, and he would slip past the press in a plain old Mini.

Freddie was obviously aware that the press were waiting outside, since you could often hear them from the bedroom. But he never knew to what extent they were there. He thought that at any one time there were no more than a handful and none of us ever corrected him. It wouldn't have helped anything.

Contrary to some newspaper reports at the time, Freddie's bedroom never became a 'mini-hospital'. He had a drip-stand at his right-hand side, in case he needed a blood transfusion, but everything else in the room was exactly as it had always been. In the last few days Freddie stopped eating solid foods; he just ate fruit and drank fruit juices.

At the end of the second week, some pictures arrived which Freddie had bought at auction but sent away for cleaning. They included the portrait of the boy he'd bought on Valentine's Day. We knew where Freddie wanted them to hang and I was left to light them properly.

The picture of the boy was for the lounge. This Freddie wanted next to the window, and I lit it with a concealed spotlight.

Mary could say some clumsy things, but perhaps she said them without really thinking. One day she suggested to me that we should ask Freddie to take his wedding ring off, as when her mother had died her fingers had swollen badly.

'The ring stays on, Mary,' I said.

Later, when I was alone with Freddie, I mentioned the idea of slipping the ring off in case his finger should swell up, but didn't say any more.

'No,' he said. 'I'm keeping it on.'

It never came off; he was even cremated with it on.

On Sunday, 17 November Freddie asked me to give his beard a trim. Whenever he asked me to trim his beard, he would pretend I was still a barber and would make an appointment.

'Ok,' I said. 'I'll do it for you on Tuesday at 10.30am.'

That Tuesday I went to his room at the allotted hour and Dave Clark was with him. Freddie looked at me and said: 'Oh, I'm sorry darling, I can't do it today. Can we do it another day?'

'Yes, all right,' I said. 'We'll do it tomorrow, same time.'

I returned the next morning and Dave was with him again. But this time Freddie wanted to go ahead with the beard trim.

When I'd finished he said: 'You know, I haven't had a bath for a few days.'

'Don't worry,' I said. 'We'll soon fix that.'

Having a real bath would have been too much of an ordeal for him by this stage. So I went downstairs and found Peter. 'I think it's time he had a good wash,' I said. So Phoebe returned with me to Freddie's room to prepare the bed.

As Freddie's skin was a little dry it was to be an oil bath. Mary came in while we were in the middle of it. She could see what was going on and decided to make herself scarce. Just as she was leaving she turned around and looked at Freddie, saying: 'Do you know what? You've got the cheekiest, impish look on your face. Aren't you sorry now you didn't get them to do this long ago?'

Freddie thoroughly enjoyed the bath and it seemed to

perk him up. His face was a picture: an innocent but cheeky childish expression all over it. We left him chatting happily with Dave. By this time Freddie was beginning to spend more time listening and less talking.

One paper claimed he'd asked Dave to ensure that his music never died, but it wasn't true. He didn't need to. Freddie was confident his music would stand the test of time. He listened to a lot of music in those last weeks, but none of it his own. More than anything he adored listening over and over to Natalie Cole's album made up of old love songs. Freddie liked them because they were so familiar to him; they were familiar to me, too. One day he was playing the album and when it got to the track 'Mona Lisa' I started singing along.

'You know this one?' he asked me.

'Of course I do,' I said. 'I know all the old ones.'

Then he listened to me singing and came up with the funniest of ideas.

'We should have recorded a song together!' he said.

The morning of Thursday, 21 November was a very sad day for me. It was the last time Freddie appeared at his bedroom window calling 'cooee', and I knew the end was very near.

That night I took special care of him. He dozed and I lay next to him on top of the bed. He only had to elbow me gently and I'd be awake if he wanted anything.

When dawn broke I was already wide awake, quietly watching television. Freddie was still asleep, cuddled inside my arm and holding on to my hand. Every so often he'd softly squeeze it. 'Do you love me?' he asked when he woke. More than ever he wanted to hear how much he was treasured. 'Yes, I love you,' I whispered and kissed him on the forehead.

At about 6.30 Freddie needed to go to the loo and I walked alongside to steady him. He sat down to have a pee and I leaned against his shoulder to support him.

'You're in the way!' he grumbled, and elbowed me painfully.

'If I move away from here you're going to fall over,' I insisted.

I got him back to bed where he sat quietly for a while. Then he just looked up to me and said: 'You know, there's something I'd love to see.'

'What is it?' I asked.

'I'd love to go down and see my pictures,' he said.

He had no control of his muscles by this time, and he couldn't even place his arms around someone's neck to support himself to be carried.

'I'll carry you,' I said. 'It's not a problem.'

Freddie sat on the bed for another five minutes summoning up his strength, then his brown eyes twinkled and he said: 'OK, let's go.'

He was wearing a Mickey Mouse dressing gown and was barefoot. Although I said I would carry him, he was adamant that he would at least try to walk as far as he could. He supported himself on the banister and stumbled down the staircase. I kept slightly ahead of him, putting my arm out to steady him. He kept pushing my arm away. It was a typical act of defiance.

When he got to the bottom of the stairs Freddie looked around the hallway at some prints Peter had rehung there. He sighed gently, looking at them for a few moments.

'Wow, they look great,' he said.

Then I led Freddie into the lounge and sat him on a chair. He sat with the newly arrived portrait of the young boy immediately ahead of him in the darkness.

One by one, I slowly flicked on the light over each picture, left to right around the room. Finally I lit up the portrait of the boy. The light fell mostly on the face, then spilled over the boy's clothes.

'They're beautiful,' said Freddie. But most of all he was mesmerised by the boy. He let out a succession of small, contented sighs. After ten minutes he announced: 'OK, let's go.' I carried him back upstairs and it was a bit of a struggle. As we reached the door he said: 'You know, I never realised you were so strong.'

'Yes, you did,' I said. He knew from our early nightclub days when I'd hurl him around the crowded dance floor. I think he said it as his way of thanking me for looking after him.

When I went back downstairs to switch off the lights I looked around the pictures slowly, soaking them in. I think that Friday morning was the last time I could honestly say Freddie was happy, the last time that Freddie Mercury was still there, the last time he radiated that Freddie Mercury excitement.

The rest of that morning he seemed alert and well aware of what was going on. Jim Beach arrived for a private meeting, and it triggered a flurry of activity to do with Freddie's statement to the press that he was suffering from Aids. I've always been very doubtful that Freddie made that statement of his own accord. He'd kept it all quiet for so long it seemed odd that he'd suddenly want to start confessing things as if he had something to be ashamed of. I'm sure he felt his fate should not become a matter for public debate. It was only a matter for him and his immediate friends. And I'm sure he didn't want to risk Joe and me being subjected to the publicity. I did not even know that Freddie was going to issue a statement.

I believe Freddie was coerced into making the statement. However, once he had been persuaded I know that Freddie specifically told Jim Beach to release the statement worldwide to prevent the British gutter press from having a scoop to themselves. It was Freddie's way of saying to those so eagerly awaiting his death: 'Fuck the lot of you!'

That Friday I slipped out for a relaxing drink at the Gate Club in Notting Hill. When I got home I went straight up to Freddie's room. He was asleep and Peter was dozing next to him on top of the bed covers.

He dozed through much of the next day, and in the

evening I went up to see him. We were lying together on the bed when he asked me what time it was.

'It's eight o'clock,' I said.

'Soon the whole world will know,' he sighed, looking at me with sad, brown eyes. This was the first indication I had that something was going on.

When Freddie nodded off I went downstairs and mentioned what he'd said to Joe and Peter. They confirmed that a statement explaining his condition had been prepared. It was due to be released at midnight.

I wasn't supposed to be keeping watch over Freddie through Saturday night – Joe was. But he'd gone out to the gym, then out for a drink, and didn't reappear. I was with Freddie in his room at around ten when he got terribly agitated. He kept asking me where Joe had got to.

'Why, what's the problem?' I asked.

'Well, I have to take my medicine,' he said.

'Oh, that's not a problem,' I answered. 'I can give you the pills you want. Which ones are they?' He knew exactly which three or four pills he needed – the painkillers. He had been taking AZT, but had abandoned the treatment along with the rest.

Freddie and I chatted away all night. I don't remember what we wittered to each other about, even when Freddie was well. It was all happy, inconsequential stuff. We didn't watch television any more. We just lay on the bed cuddling until he dozed off. And sometimes so did I.

Occasionally he gave me a quick jab to the ribs to stop me snoring, or a harder one if he needed something. Then he asked me to prepare some fruit for him in the kitchen. I sliced some mango and added a little sorbet to help fight his chronic dehydration.

We drifted asleep again. When Freddie next woke me it was about three and he seemed incapable of explaining himself. He couldn't talk properly and kept pointing to his mouth, frowning. Something was terribly wrong. I tried to work out what he wanted, but couldn't.

About half an hour later Joe came back home and saw I was having problems. As soon as Freddie spotted Joe, he pointed to his mouth.

'What is it, Freddie?' Joe asked. 'What do you want?'

I told him this had been going on for half an hour, ever since I had prepared some fruit for Freddie which he'd then eaten before dozing off.

Joe leaned over Freddie and opened his mouth. A piece of mango had lodged at the back of his throat which he could neither swallow nor bring back up. Joe prised Freddie's jaw open wide and flicked out the offending piece of fruit with his finger. Freddie didn't say anything. Joe and I were fully aware that a healthy Freddie would have been furious with me for not understanding. He sipped some juice, then went back to sleep.

I went downstairs for a coffee, followed closely by Joe. He was about to apologise for not having turned up for night duty, but I wouldn't let him speak.

'Don't worry about it,' I said. I guess I knew where Joe had got to. It was a very heavy strain to bear; he'd found it all too much that day and had had to get away from Garden Lodge to forget about Freddie for a while.

Joe went upstairs to Freddie's room and lay next to him on the bed. A few minutes later I went back, told Joe to get some sleep and took his place next to Freddie, who was fast asleep.

Freddie woke up again at six in the morning and uttered what were to be his last two words: 'Pee, pee!' He wanted to be helped to the loo. He looked terribly weak and I had to carry him. As I lowered him back on to the bed I heard a deafening crack. It sounded like one of Freddie's bones breaking, cracking like the branch of a tree. He screamed out in pain and went into a convulsion.

I yelled for Joe. I needed him to pin Freddie to the bed to stop him injuring himself. Over the years Joe had seen Freddie have one anxiety attack after another and he knew just how to handle him – by pinning him down until the anxiety had passed. He said: 'Freddie, calm down. Freddie, calm down.' Then Freddie's hand shot up and went straight for Joe's throat. He was like a drowning man clutching for air.

Joe freed himself from Freddie's grip and eventually he calmed him down. Then, exhausted by the strain, Freddie promptly fell asleep. We phoned his GP, Dr Gordon Atkinson, and he came over and gave Freddie an injection of morphine to help him through the day. Joe later told me Freddie was allergic to morphine, but it was now so late in the day it didn't seem to matter.

Mary came by later in the morning and we all stood around in the kitchen, waiting to hear Dr Atkinson's prognosis. He said: 'Freddie will probably last until Thursday.'

Joe and I looked at each other. We both knew that there was no way Freddie could last that long.

Mary left shortly after that. The rest of that day Freddie nodded in and out of sleep. Elton John came to visit him one last time, driving himself in his green Bentley. He parked right outside the gate, blocking Logan Road completely. His attitude to the press was 'Stuff you lot. I want to see my friend and I don't care about any of you.' He didn't stay very long.

I felt the need to get well away from Garden Lodge, so that afternoon I took myself off in the Volvo to Holland Park where I moped around for an hour.

By the time I got back, Freddie was as ill as I'd ever seen him. He seemed to know what was going on around him, but couldn't respond to any of it; he could hear, but couldn't move his eyes to acknowledge he'd heard. He just stared straight ahead, eyes glazed.

Dr Atkinson stayed at the house all afternoon and left just after 6.30. I thanked him for having stayed so long, saw him out, and then went straight back to be with Freddie.

All that day Delilah had been in the bedroom, but not once had she sat on the bed; she remained crouched at the foot. Dave Clark was sitting by the bed, massaging Freddie's hand. I picked Delilah up and placed her next to Freddie. Dave then took Freddie's hand and started stroking Delilah's coat with it.

'It's Delilah,' he told Freddie. He seemed to recognise what he was being told.

Freddie made clear he wanted to go to the loo. After the terrible convulsions which had followed his morning visit to the bathroom, I wasn't bold enough to try to cope with him again single-handed. I flew downstairs and found Phoebe.

By the time we got back upstairs, Freddie had wet the bed. Dave Clark didn't seem to have noticed.

Peter looked over at me and asked: 'Shall we change the bedclothes?'

'We'd better,' I answered. 'If we don't and he wakes up he'll go absolutely ape-shit.'

I don't know why I said that; perhaps it was my subconscious trying to make out that things were less serious than they were.

Peter started changing the bed while I took care of Freddie. As I was about to change Freddie into a clean T-shirt and pair of boxer shorts, I asked Dave to leave the room for a few moments.

It was when I was getting his shorts on that I felt him try to raise his left leg to help a little. It was the last thing he did. I looked down at him, knowing he was dead.

'Phoebe,' I cried out. 'I'm sorry, he's gone.'

I slipped my arm under Freddie's neck, kissed him and then held him. His eyes were still open. I can remember very clearly the expression on his face – and when I go to sleep every night it's still there in front of me. He looked radiant. One minute he was a boy with a gaunt, sad little face and the next he was a picture of ecstasy. Freddie's whole face went back to everything it had been before. He looked finally and totally at peace. Seeing him like that made me feel happy in my sadness. I felt an overwhelming sense of relief. I knew that he was no longer in pain.

Dave Clark had only got as far as the doorway when

Freddie died. He came back in to stay with me, and Phoebe ran to find Joe.

I stopped the tiny fly-wheel of the wind-up carriage clock by the bed. I'd given it to Freddie because he told me he'd always wanted one. It read twelve minutes to seven. I've never started it again.

11

NO ESCAPE FROM REALITY

A few minutes after Freddie died on that November night in 1991, Joe ran into the room looking for a mirror to see if there was any sign of breathing.

'Look,' I said softly. 'He's gone.'

Joe ran out into The Mews, screaming: 'Where's the doctor?' He was almost in tears.

We crossed Freddie's arms and put a little teddy in his hands. It had been sent by a well-wisher and seemed appropriate.

Mary was the first to be phoned, then the doctor was reached in his car and started to make his way back. Mary telephoned Freddie's parents and sister and broke the news to them.

A lot of things that went on in the hours immediately following Freddie's death are no more than a blur to me. I didn't know what planet I was on.

I went downstairs to switch off the lights in the garden for a few seconds, then slipped off to my room to ring my mother in Ireland. As soon as she answered, I began crying uncontrollably. She couldn't make out a word I was saying. I asked her: 'Could you phone the bishop and ask him to say a mass for Freddie?'

She said: 'Calm down, son.' I took a few moments to compose myself. 'Now,' she said. 'What's happened?'

'Freddie died,' I said. There was nothing she could say to

console me, but she tried. She asked me to tell her exactly how it had happened and I did. I needed to tell someone who would understand. When I rang off I stayed in my room for a while, trying to hold back the tears.

When I rejoined the others, Phoebe was trying to contact Jim Beach by telephone. He had flown to Los Angeles after seeing Freddie on Friday. Then Dr Atkinson returned.

I went back into Freddie's room and stood looking at him. When the two of us were left alone for a moment, I said a little prayer. Then I looked at him and said aloud: 'You bastard! Well, at least you're free now. The press can't hurt you any more.'

About half an hour after Freddie died, Mary came to pay her last respects. She stayed for ten minutes. When Joe and Phoebe came into the room, the four of us had a big hug. This was our hour of need and we all turned to Phoebe. He'd lost his mother recently and he seemed to know how to cope. Only Joe, Phoebe and I knew just how exhausting it had been nursing Freddie for nights on end, watching helplessly as his health deteriorated dramatically, witnessing the ravages of his cruel and unremitting illness.

Later that evening Freddie's parents arrived and went to his bedside. Freddie looked so serene, ecstatic and radiant that they asked whether we had put make-up on his face. We said we hadn't.

All of us at Garden Lodge knew what arrangements Freddie would have wanted when he died. We didn't need instruction on this from him; we just knew. His body was to be taken out of the house as quickly as possible. Phoebe's father was a retired undertaker and everything was handled by his former company. Usually undertakers take away the body in a bag, placed in a tin box. We all agreed that this was not good enough for Freddie. We insisted he had to leave in a proper oak coffin.

We'd planned that Freddie's body would leave Garden Lodge at the stroke of midnight. His body was to be driven to a secret location – in fact a chapel of rest in Ladbroke

Grove, west London. But Phoebe had such difficulty raising Jim Beach in America that it held up Freddie's departure. Actually, when he did reach him, around midnight, Jim Beach asked whether the body could be kept at Garden Lodge until the next day, giving him time to fly home to accompany it as it left the house. Phoebe and I vetoed the idea.

News of Freddie's death reached the press twenty minutes before his body left Garden Lodge at 12.20am. But the body was taken out in an anonymous van and the police did a brilliant job preventing photographers and reporters from following it.

It was pandemonium outside Garden Lodge the following day. Freddie's death made headlines around the globe and the press were frantic to know exactly when he'd died and what he looked like. When the phone rang in the house, I just didn't want to know; I left it to Phoebe or Joe to deal with.

Flowers started arriving from Freddie's fans all over the world and Joe, Phoebe, Terry and myself took turns to bring in the constant stream of bouquets and wreaths from the gate. Eventually the Queen office enlisted some security lads to help us.

The more the flowers kept coming, the more I felt myself cracking up without Freddie around. In the end I ran around the house and collected every single music video of Freddie I could find. Then I sat down, surrounded by the cats, and watched them over and over again, bawling my head off. It helped a great deal, and over the next fortnight I would watch them for hours on end. I'd sob my heart out on the sofa, cuddling the cats for comfort. And if I went out, on my Walkman or car cassette player I'd listen to the *Mr Bad Guy* album that Freddie had given me in the first year we were together.

In the title track, 'Mr Bad Guy', one line made the hairs on the back of my neck stand on end each time it came round: 'Yes, I'm everybody's Mr Bad Guy – can't you see, I'm Mr Mercury, spread your wings and fly away with me.' To me, Freddie was always one of the good guys. When I heard the song I was cheered that we had flown off together until our wings were cruelly clipped.

The three of us at Garden Lodge dealt with Freddie's death in our own ways. Phoebe stayed in the kitchen, watching endless television. Joe channelled his grief into work-outs at the gym, but he had taken it terribly badly and almost went to pieces. When he came back from the gym that first day, he couldn't handle me playing Freddie's videos and stormed into the kitchen. He asked Phoebe at the top of his voice: 'Why's he playing all Freddie's music?'

Joe went off to his room and came to realise that I was simply doing my own thing, finding my equivalent of going to a gym. He cooled down, and in the harrowing nights which followed he became a real soulmate.

On that Monday night, just one day after Freddie's death, I went out alone to drown my sorrows. I walked to the Gate Club in Notting Hill intending to get totally legless. As I walked through the door Bobby, one of the bar staff, said: 'Jim, you look very depressed.'

'Yes,' I said. 'My boyfriend just died.' I mentioned that my partner was Freddie, but I don't think anyone believed me. At the end of the night, drunk and emotionally drained, I walked slowly back to Garden Lodge. I found a friend in a total stranger, a lone fan outside Garden Lodge gate, beside himself with grief and crying his head off.

I tried to comfort him and we talked for a long time about how wonderful Freddie was. I hung on his every word of praise for Freddie and I guess he thought I was just another fan driven to pilgrimage. In a way he was right.

When a black cab pulled up in Logan Place, a dark figure got out; it was a woman who was as drunk as a skunk. She tottered past us and as she did she slurred something in our direction, but we had no idea what she had said. Five minutes later the same black figure approached us again. She had made us each a mug of piping hot cocoa. It was an unexpected and kind gesture on such a chilly night.

As we sipped the warming drinks, the woman said most coherently: 'You know, I've lived here a long time but I've never actually seen Freddie Mercury – though I've always been aware he was here.'

We talked for a while longer and then I said: 'Well, I'm sorry. I've got to go to bed now.' I got up and stuck my key in the lock.

'What is this?' she asked. 'Is this some kind of trick?'

'What do you mean?' I said.

'How come you're opening the gate?' she asked.

'I live here,' I said.

The poor fan just didn't know what to do. I invited the two of them into the garden to see the vast patch-work of colourful floral tributes covering the lawn. We talked for a little longer before they left and I went to bed.

On Tuesday morning flowers began arriving again at dawn, and again we ran shifts on the gate to ferry them inside the grounds. We didn't leave one stem outside on the pavement; every flower came in and every flower went on the five hearses for the funeral the following day. We weren't sure what we could do with all the flowers after the funeral service, but in the end Phoebe came up with the answer: they were shipped to every Aids hospice, hospital and old people's home in the area.

Flowers were so important to Freddie that I wanted to send something appropriate. Reminded of his beloved swans on the lake in Montreux, I sent him a swan in white flowers. The message on the card I chose was a few lines from a remembrance card for my father when he had died almost a decade earlier:

Others were taken, yes I know
But you were mine, I loved you so.
A prayer, a tear till the end of time,
For a loving friend I was proud to call mine.
To a beautiful life, a sad, sad end,
You died as you lived, everyone's friend.

The morning of Freddie's cremation, Wednesday, 27 November 1991, was grey and overcast. I woke up in a dreadful state. As I got dressed I realised that I was going down with another heavy bout of flu. It wasn't a good start to a terrible day.

The funeral service was at two in the afternoon at the West London Crematorium. But even on that day of all days, our last private moments were taken from us. At Jim Beach's invitation, paparazzi photographer Richard Young was at Garden Lodge to take intimate pictures both before and after the service.

One lovely gesture, carried out to the letter, was suggested by Joe, who said we should each wear the Butler and Wilson's jewellery Freddie had given us for Christmas 1989. 'He would have liked that,' he said. 'It's a bit of glit, isn't it?' We all agreed.

Until then I'd never worn the massive cut-glass and silver tie-pin Freddie had given me. All around the world they talk of wearing your ribbon with pride; well, that day I wore my tie-pin with pride.

It had been agreed some time before that it would be appropriate for Mary and me to travel together in the first car in the funeral procession. As we prepared to leave Garden Lodge for the service, for the first time Mary metaphorically slapped me in the face. She said she didn't want me in the first car – she wanted Dave Clark. I was very hurt.

When we left the house Mary and Dave took the first car, Jim Beach went in the second, while Joe, Phoebe and I shared the third. The three of us felt let down. We'd been the ones with Freddie through thick and thin during his illness, and it seemed that no sooner was he dead than we were being pushed aside.

In the small chapel of rest, Freddie's family sat on the right with the rest of us on the left. I was a little heartened to see Mary sitting in the front row waiting for the three of us to sit with her. Dave Clark must have realised the cruel way Mary had spurned me on this of all days and he slipped into one of the pews behind us. We spoke to Freddie's parents before joining Mary. We all found the service difficult, and I made a point of holding Mary's hand from beginning to end of the service.

Freddie's faith was one of the world's oldest: Zoroastrianism. The service was therefore an unusual one, conducted by priests in white robes chanting traditional prayers that I didn't understand. So I said my own prayers and mentally held my own service for Freddie. When he was alive we had never spoken about our beliefs; I'm sure he guessed I was a Catholic. But while he was alive, as long as we had each other nothing else seemed to matter.

Brian, Roger and John were there, and so was Elton John. Afterwards Brian and I shook hands and he said how nice it was to see me and how very sorry he was about Freddie's death. Roger said the same, and rather than shake hands we hugged. I was very pleased to see John at the funeral and told him so and thanked him. He'd kept his distance as Freddie was fading away, but came to pay his last respects. We shook hands and had a little cuddle. The only other conversation I can remember from that day was with the black cemetery moggie.

The service was followed by a small reception at Garden Lodge, which was still being besieged by the press. Jim Beach thought it right to let people come back to the house after the service if they wanted to. Brian, Roger and John went straight out for a quiet lunch together instead. Elton didn't come back, but Freddie's doctors did.

This may seem glum, but I'd rather hoped that at Garden Lodge we'd talk quietly about how the service had gone and generally remember Freddie with a little reverence and dignity. Instead it was party time. Horrendous, shrill laughter came from the kitchen and it tore me apart.

As the first champagne cork popped that afternoon I found myself drifting away from the others. I felt disgusted at what I thought of as disrespect for Freddie that day. I'm sure Freddie would have loved a massive champagne party thrown to send him on his way, but that wasn't what it seemed. Perhaps if we'd all gone off somewhere for lunch, like the band, it might have been easier to have a celebratory farewell for Freddie. But it didn't happen; instead we gave him a surreal send-off.

The sound of the shrieking laughter that day still haunts me. I just couldn't stand it, so I took myself off to sit in Number 27 bus shelter with Delilah and Goliath for company and comfort. Every so often I'd glance up at Freddie's bedroom window and each time I pictured him there, looking at me and calling 'Cooee'. I was in a very quiet mood and so lost in my own world that I've no idea what happened in the rest of that awful afternoon or at what time people started to drift away.

Phoebe, Joe and I did not sit down right away to have a discussion about our future; that was something we'd have to do in our own time, when things were quieter and we'd had a while to come to terms with Freddie's death. For the time being we planned to keep going just as we were, as if Freddie was simply away on tour.

Then Joe suggested that he wouldn't be staying in the house very much longer, as with no Freddie to cook for he had no job to do. More importantly, he was aware that his own time was fast running out. He wanted to go back to America. Of course, Phoebe's job as Freddie's assistant was also defunct, but he had no immediate plans.

Jim Beach gave the three of us plenty of reassurance that day. He was the executor of Freddie's will and knew his last wishes.

Joe asked him, 'What's going to happen to us now?'

'Well,' Jim replied, 'as you know, Freddie's wishes are that you are to stay in this house as long as you want.'

'Yes,' we all said. 'We know that.'

We also knew that Freddie would be leaving the bulk of his estate to Mary, including the house, and Jim confirmed this. He also mentioned what was relevant to us in the will, namely that we'd each receive a tax-free sum of £500,000. 'My god, so much!' Phoebe blurted out, echoing my thoughts exactly. The three of us were very much taken by surprise.

I thought that Freddie might maybe leave a few thousand to me, but not half as much as this. I discovered later that when he spoke to friends about our fate after he'd gone, he would say: 'They will be looked after. They will never have to work again.'

Then Joe asked another question of particular relevance to him and me. Freddie had led us to believe that once he had died our medical bills would be looked after by his estate. I know he expected this; though I'd never asked, he always insisted on paying my medical bills. Joe was terribly anxious, as he was already undergoing private Aids medication. Jim Beach promised nothing, but told us he'd see what he could do.

I was still battling with my flu and, after the guests had left, I went to lie on the couch in the lounge with a duvet over me and the gas fire on full blast. I was so cold I was shivering, yet I was also sweating. I felt I was burning up.

There were still three or four of Freddie's doctors in the house and Joe turned to them to demand: 'For Christ's sake, can't any of you do anything for Jim?' But it was a heavy cold and there was nothing they could offer me. Joe insisted on finding two sleeping tablets for me and helping me off to bed. I swallowed them and may have slept for about half an hour before I was wide awake again. My mind just wouldn't stop buzzing.

I remembered so many wonderful times I'd enjoyed with Freddie. On some occasions I had to share him with thousands of others, but there were often times when it was just the two of us for nights on end. A million images flowed through my mind, each one of him either laughing his socks off or looking as soft and vulnerable as a rose petal.

By four in the morning, my mind was still exploding into colourful memories of our time together. I remembered Freddie's looks of surprise each time a new kitten joined the team, or his happiness when feeding his pet koi. I flew around the world, seeing flashbacks of Japan, Ibiza, Barcelona, Montreux and Hungary. Eventually my mind collapsed, and I crashed into a short but heavy sleep.

When I got up the following morning I made my way to the kitchen, where Joe asked how I'd slept. I told him my mind had been on overdrive all night with memories of Freddie, and I'd barely slept at all.

'You didn't take both tablets, did you?' he asked.

'I did, yes,' I said.

'You should only have taken one,' he said, slightly alarmed. 'That's what they do if you take too many. They're like speed!'

I slept in Freddie's bedroom for a few nights, even though the room felt totally empty without him. I'd lie on top of the bed, either crying or just smiling about nothing. I never actually got into bed; I think that would have cracked me apart. I dreaded waking up in the room and finding him not there. More than once I hoped for a split second that it had all been just a lousy dream, but I soon returned to reality, a living nightmare.

On Thursday morning, I got up to ferry flowers once more from outside the gate into the garden and talk to some of Freddie's fans who'd turned up to pay their respects. They seemed to be arriving from everywhere – Britain, Japan, America. At least the press had left.

The three of us arranged, with Mary, that that year we should all spend Christmas together one last time at Garden Lodge – along with Piers and baby Richard, Dave Clark and Trevor Clarke. Then, exactly a week after Freddie's cremation and our first meeting with Jim Beach, we were summoned to a second meeting, also held in the house. This time it was with Jim Beach the tough-nosed businessman.

He came straight to the point. A week earlier he'd reassured us by explaining that he knew it was Freddie's wish that we stayed at Garden Lodge as long as we liked. However, that day Jim told us: 'As you know, Freddie's wishes were that you should live here as long as you like. But unfortunately he didn't write them in the will, so they're not legally binding.' Mary was receiving the bulk of Freddie's estate, including, as expected, ownership of Garden Lodge.

'Uh-oh,' I thought to myself. 'Wait for it!'

Jim continued: 'So, you are going to be given three months' notice to leave to find yourselves alternative accommodation. We are going to get some money released for you, to tide you over in the meantime.' I assume he was saying that for my benefit, knowing that for seven years my home had been Freddie's and I had nowhere else in London to go. An advance would at least allow me to raise a deposit quickly to buy somewhere to live. It was a foregone conclusion Mary would soon be moving into the house with Piers and their son Richard. The only good news that day was that we would continue to be paid until our final day at Garden Lodge.

The date set for our departure is engraved on my mind: Sunday, 1 March. It hung over me like a cloud from then on, and also marked the date from which Mary's attitude to me changed dramatically.

Three weeks after Freddie's death, in tribute to Freddie and to raise money for Aids causes, Queen's biggest song, 'Bohemian Rhapsody', was rush-released and went straight to Number One. It meant that everywhere I turned I heard Freddie singing. I wished until it hurt that he was still around, but there was no escape from reality.

I returned to the Gate Club one night and spoke to a mate who worked there. Since my last visit they must have seen me in the paper because they all seemed to know I really was Freddie's boyfriend. I was propping up the bar with a pint in front of me, when out of the blue the first chords of 'A Kind of Magic' struck up and the video filled the monitors with pictures of Freddie. A split second later the song and the video had been turned off. James, one of the managers, came flying over to me to apologise for being so insensitive.

'Don't be stupid,' I said. 'Put it on.' With another flicker Freddie's face was on every screen.

I supped my drink, lit a cigarette and looked around to see everyone enjoying the music. 'That's my man,' I thought happily.

I decided to go home to Ireland for a week, to be with my family. I was slightly anxious about returning, as the *Sunday Mirror* had just rerun a story revealing me as Freddie's boyfriend. It meant that there was a serious risk of the papers coming after me to find a gruesome new angle on Freddie's death for their front pages.

As I left for the trip, Mary too was leaving Garden Lodge. In an odd and thoughtless attempt to try to cheer me up she said: 'Freddie's probably waiting for you already.' It was a very cruel remark to make to someone who would inevitably share Freddie's fate.

As it happened, I didn't have any problems with the press in Ireland. I went back with my eldest brother, Johnny, after attending my niece's nursing passing-out presentation at Wembley Stadium. During the ceremony a lump came to my throat when it was announced that a bouquet was to be sent to the Ealing College of Art in memory of one of its most famous students – Freddie Mercury. Then, when they called for a minute's silence in memory of Freddie, I had a silent sob to myself.

My first night at home in Ireland I turned in at about ten in the evening and quickly fell into a deep sleep. Four hours later I woke from the most sublime dream; I was floating all alone in a tunnel of feathers, talking to Freddie. I went downstairs, beaming a wide smile, and discovered my mother, who keeps very odd hours, in the kitchen.

'What are you looking so happy about?' she asked, and I

told her all about my dream. After a cup of tea I went back to bed, but couldn't recapture the dream. And time and again since then I have tried to find Freddie in my dreams, but I only receive brief flashes of him.

I decided on that visit that I would concentrate my mind and energies into decorating my mum's home. One day Phoebe phoned, suggesting that it might be a good idea if I spent Christmas with my family in Ireland.

'No,' I said, not realising that he was trying to tell me I was not wanted at Garden Lodge any more. I was adamant. 'I've decided I am going to spend Christmas in Garden Lodge anyway,' I said.

When I got back to London I was greeted by a solemn-looking Phoebe. He told me: 'We are no longer sleeping in Garden Lodge. We've all been moved to The Mews.' From now on Garden Lodge was to be opened each day to allow the three of us to go about our business, but every night at six it was to be locked. No one was allowed to sleep in the house overnight. And the house alarm system was being increased tenfold.

So I had come home to discover I didn't have a home any more. It was such a mean-spirited thing to do and very depressing for all of us. I told Phoebe how chilly the atmosphere had become since Freddie had died, and he agreed.

'I might as well go to a hotel or get a flat,' I said. 'The Mews has nothing to do with me. All my memories of Freddie are in the house.'

Next I learned what had caused the change. One day while I was in Ireland the house had been left unattended and without the alarm on. This wasn't quite true. On the night in question Joe had been in the house, and Phoebe was sleeping in The Mews. Joe had arranged to meet friends for breakfast and left the house at around eight-thirty in the morning. Phoebe was due in half an hour, so Joe locked up but didn't bother to flick on the alarm. Before Phoebe arrived, Mary had found the house unalarmed and phoned

Jim Beach about it. Jim then told Joe and Phoebe that the three of us were banished to The Mews until we were off the premises completely.

I was devastated by what was happening to us. I know Freddie would have been furious. Garden Lodge, once a place of such warmth and care, was now about to resemble Fort Knox.

Some of Queen's security lads were drafted in to provide a twenty-four-hour guard over the property. We knew them all and they hung around with us in The Mews. They'd known Garden Lodge under Freddie and couldn't understand what was going on. One of the lads in particular, Sean, asked: 'What the hell is all this?' I didn't tell him, but the answer was that it was just one person's doing and the result of one person's paranoia.

Instead of being in quiet mourning, Garden Lodge was filled with strangers, drilling holes and ripping the place apart to install the cabling for countless cameras to protect the property from Freddie's fans. There were still flowers in the house, although no one except the workmen was really there to enjoy them any more. Many of these blooms had been left at the gate by fans, passing by the gate to pay their last respects. Little did they know that, on the other side of the wall, Freddie's wonderful world had all but disappeared.

I did receive a very kind letter from Freddie's mum. She thanked me for loving Freddie and looking after him so well. They were kind words and I appreciated them very much.

As we thought, it was confirmed that once we had moved out, Mary would be taking up residence in Garden Lodge herself, with Piers and their baby son. We were told that the 'family' Christmas lunch was still going ahead as planned, but it too would be banished to The Mews. We felt another kick in the stomach. Moreover, Joe wouldn't be there. Mary told Phoebe and me in no uncertain terms that she didn't like him. She also said that once he had left Garden Lodge he would never set foot in it again. They were harsh words about someone who had been so loyal and kind to Freddie throughout his illness.

The only nice thing to happen around that time was an invitation from Elton John for the three of us to visit him in his beautiful home in Old Windsor for a Boxing Day party. We were a bit concerned as to who would drive as it would be quite a party, but Elton had thoughtfully taken care of that; a car was laid on for us.

I wasn't looking forward to Christmas. I thought: no Freddie – no Christmas. I'd got so despondent I decided I wouldn't even bother with a tree or decorations, but Phoebe talked me around. In the end I got a small tree, but when it was dressed up it looked like a twig compared to the trees we'd always had at Garden Lodge.

As Joe was not invited, on Christmas Day Phoebe prepared the small Christmas lunch in the Garden Lodge kitchen and ferried it over to The Mews. We tried so hard to be jocular, but we didn't feel comfortable. We were all painfully aware that the one person who had made our Christmas for so long was missing. For me the day was awkward and the atmosphere thin. We swapped presents – Phoebe, Mary, Piers, Richard and so on – but it wasn't a bit enjoyable. Freddie would have hated it all, too. I know he would have wanted us to spend Christmas in the house. Still, under the circumstances we did our best to make it a special day. Dave Clark and Trevor Clarke made flying visits to see how we were getting on.

Elton's party on Boxing Day was a welcome break from the Garden Lodge nightmare. His home is a country mansion set in acres of fabulous lush countryside. Ever the perfect host, he had laid on a huge buffet. At first I found the party thoroughly enjoyable; then – and I mean no disrespect to Elton – I began to find it hard going. There were maybe twenty or thirty very nice people there, but I knew very few of them. I'd never been involved in the music business; my place had only been at Freddie's side. One friendly face there was Tony King, who asked how I was. This was a social occasion, not a time to moan, so I told him I was shaky at times but generally fine.

But when Elton swapped Christmas presents with his guests, I became very sad. What should have been the happiest of scenes simply reminded me how much I missed Freddie and his heartfelt joy at giving presents at Christmas-time. I slipped out of the house and went for a walk, strolling in the grounds until I came across two lovable ponies. I stayed with them, popping into the house every so often to find apples to feed them.

Even among so many people, it was an agonisingly lonely day for me. I just couldn't mix. By about eight in the evening the guests were starting to leave, but I didn't want to go anywhere. Having spent a while in such surroundings and been looked after so well, the thought of going back to The Mews meant nothing to me. I'd be returning to a void. I hated returning to The Mews when all my happiest memories of Freddie were locked up in Garden Lodge.

Elton's manager John Reid was in his car waiting to say goodbye to me. 'Look, Jim,' he said. 'If there's ever anything you need, let us know.' I assumed that by *us* he meant him and Elton. It was a kind thought, but Phoebe, Joe and I were never ones to make ourselves a nuisance.

When we got home I found The Mews so uninviting that I headed off to the pub. The next morning I stood in the doorway staring up at Freddie's bedroom window. 'Cooee' came into my mind, and a few tears came into my eyes.

The only regular visitors to The Mews in all that time were the cats. Miko slept with me every night and Romeo came for sanctuary from the madness in the house.

I went out for New Year. I thought Freddie would have done, so if only for him I should, too. It was a disastrous night, a desperate party of a friend of a friend.

Early in the New Year, Mary offered the three of us the chance to take from Garden Lodge any presents we'd given Freddie. Our initial response was instinctive, a resounding 'No'. These were things we'd bought Freddie; they were a part of him and a part of the Garden Lodge he had built from scratch. Each had its own special place in our hearts and his house. But Mary returned to the subject a few days later when we were all in the kitchen. She explained that in order to find the upkeep for the house she might be forced to sell off certain things. First to go would be the presents that we had bought Freddie, unless we took them away.

The three of us shot each other the same telling look. We still felt our presents should stay along with Freddie's other treasures. There was no risk that Freddie had left Mary struggling, so there would be no need to sell things. She was just trying to chase us away. We knew she was clearly telling us something that day. She knew that each of the things we'd given Freddie held cherished memories of our loving times with him. Each present was special. She was telling us that none of that mattered any more.

As much as we wanted to refuse the return of the presents, we eventually accepted defeat. Further discussion was pointless, and we didn't wanted our things flung from the house. So we each soberly looked around, reclaiming some of the presents we'd once given with so much warmth and love. At the end of the day we all left a lot of things behind.

The one piece of furniture I took from Garden Lodge was a couch in the Japanese Room which Freddie had given me for our retreat in Ireland. But I deliberately left behind the two little tables that Freddie had asked me to make for him for the bedroom. I felt they were special and belonged to that special room.

I am certain Freddie had never intended me to be ousted from what he'd always asked me to consider as *our* home. I'm also convinced he'd expected me to continue looking after the cats. If my circumstances changed and I had to move from Garden Lodge, he would assume I'd do so with some of the cats. I asked Mary if I could take Miko with me. The answer was short and to the point. No. Technically Joe, too, was entitled to Goliath and Delilah, and he spoke to me about looking after them for him. But we were firmly put in our place about the cats. None of them would be leaving. Then I was told I might be allowed to take Goliath, but only if Goliath didn't get on with Mary's baby son when she moved in. Goliath was allergic to children, so there was a chance he wouldn't settle down. I never heard about it again.

On 6 February, Freddie was posthumously honoured at the British Phonographic Industry's 'Brits' awards. Joe, Phoebe and I weren't invited. The Queen organisation clearly didn't deem us close enough to Freddie to ask us to be there. It was cruel of them; I watched it on television instead.

That day I was in the Garden Lodge kitchen with Mary. I still wonder whether what she said then was because her conscience was beginning to prick her.

'Jim,' she said, 'I've been thinking. Maybe you can stay on in Garden Lodge until you can find yourself a place.'

'Mary,' I said, perfectly politely. 'Thank you very much. But I think you should clear that with Jim Beach first.' We said no more of it.

Next day Mary returned to the subject. 'Things are as they were,' she said and the matter was closed.

Relations between Mary and me continued to be strained. I had a collection of photographs in the house and some I wanted to have back, to remind me of my life with Freddie, but I didn't just want to help myself. When Mary and I were in Freddie's bedroom one day, I asked her if I could take the framed photographs of Freddie he had placed for me on my side of what had been our bed. She didn't reply.

In the kitchen the following morning with Mary, Joe and Terry, I asked again if she'd allow me to have the pictures on my side of the bed. Her response startled me.

She spun around and denied I'd ever asked for the photographs. She said she hadn't heard me and nor had Terry – who wasn't even there. She began asking him if he'd heard anything.

'No,' I said. 'Terry wouldn't have heard you, Mary.' She

kept on about not having heard me ask. She could be like a dog with a bone whenever she got something into her head. She was throwing a tantrum and being totally selfish. So I'm sorry to say I lost my temper.

'Mary, I've lost my friend, my lover, my home, my *life*,' I said. I stormed out into the garden. Terry and Joe were frozen in the doorway, certain that I was angry enough to hit her. In all the years they'd known me, they had not once seen me lose my temper.

In the garden I calmed down and ten minutes later went back to the kitchen. I went up to Mary and hugged her. 'I'm sorry for that outburst,' I said, but I got no response from her. It was the last time I spoke to her before I moved out.

12

LIVING ON MY OWN

As the 1 March deadline to leave The Mews loomed in 1992, I still didn't have anywhere to go. Fortunately, at the last minute a friend helped me out by offering a room in his small flat in Shepherd's Bush for a while.

Phoebe, Joe and I were then informed that Mary had arranged for someone to move in as soon as we'd gone. She needed someone to look after Garden Lodge until she could move in herself. Her new housekeeper would be arriving the very day we were to leave. This total stranger would be the first person to stay in Freddie's world since our expulsion from the house in December.

We were assured that the outsider, out of consideration for us, wouldn't arrive early; we would each be given enough time to reflect and say our farewells to our memories of Freddie. The memories still poured from every square inch of every room. Saying goodbye to Freddie's Garden Lodge was going to be difficult.

I made two or three journeys to Isleworth in Middlesex, to take some of my bits and pieces to store with friends. On one trip I felt so depressed I nearly had an accident on the motorway. I couldn't even listen to *Mr Bad Guy*; I just cried my eyes out.

As the days wore on it became evident that Mary had no intention of coming over to say goodbye to any of us in person. It was a great shame. Our last month's wages arrived in the post that final weekend – the only time they weren't delivered by Mary herself. We were also given redundancy money, in my case the equivalent of four weeks' wages. And we learned that, although the three of us returned our keys to Garden Lodge, within hours of our leaving all the locks were to be changed. It was such a sad end to such happy years of our lives.

That final Sunday morning started with the doorbell ringing at 7.30am to announce the arrival of Mary's zealous new housekeeper. There he was on the doorstep, suitcase in hand, ready to move into *his* new home. Even the promised dignity of our last morning was taken from us.

Phoebe went first, mid-morning. The farewell wasn't tearful. The time for tears had come and gone by this stage. Though we were parting company, we knew we'd always keep in touch. Joe and I hugged him and he left. There were many tears, though, when Joe left. He was flying straight to America. I helped him pack, and when it was time to go we had a long hugging session in The Mews doorway.

I decided I wouldn't leave until two in the afternoon. Apart from the alien housekeeper and Sean, the security man on duty that day, I had the place to myself for one last time. I went over to Garden Lodge and looked around wistfully.

'Jim, what about your bedroom furniture?' Sean asked.

'Well,' I replied. 'I've got nowhere to store it.' Much to my regret, I was leaving it all behind: the Biedermeier table that Freddie had designed for me, the Biedermeier bed-head dotted with his decorative ormolu designs, and the chests of drawers.

I took a slow look around the house and walked out of the front door, gazing back at Freddie's bedroom window imagining a final 'Cooee'. I went to The Mews and picked up the last of my things. Then I walked to the door, looked up to his bedroom window for the very last, lingering time, and left.

It was Mary's birthday on 6 March, so I sent flowers to

Garden Lodge. As far as I was concerned there would be was no more animosity between us: I hoped there might still be some kind of lasting friendship. I'd always promised Freddie I'd be there for Mary – always – and whether or not I remained in Garden Lodge made no difference.

It took a while to realise that I had been ousted from what was left of Freddie's life. Some nights I couldn't bear it. I was depressed, felt lost and suffered some kind of breakdown. They were bleak weeks and months. I'd walk back to Garden Lodge late at night when there was no one around and call quietly for Miko and the other cats. To my great delight, one or two would pop over the wall on hearing my voice. I'd play with them and stroke or cuddle them, often emptying my heart to them through my tears. Seeing the cats again brought me just that bit closer to Freddie. It made such a difference.

Through March, April and May I was putting myself through this ritual about four times a week. I could think of nowhere else to go or anyone better than the cats in whom I could renew memories of Freddie. I paid regular visits there right up until the first anniversary of Freddie's death in November 1992. After that the cats stopped coming when I called. I never saw them again.

The cash advance that Jim Beach promised the three of us eventually arrived, to be offset against the money we were eventually to inherit. We hoped for the £50,000 that had been promised but were given only £20,000 apiece.

On Easter Monday, 20 April 1992, the world collectively rocked to the beat of Freddie's drum with the tribute concert to him at Wembley Stadium. I ordered my ticket through the Queen office and, like everybody else there, didn't begrudge paying one bit. All the proceeds were helping Aids causes and raising public awareness of the illness.

Joe and Phoebe were there and we all had limited passes to go backstage to meet Brian, Roger and John in the interval. It was the first time I'd seen them since the cremation and they were very welcoming and friendly.

As I stood among the 72,000-strong crowd for the second half of the spectacular, I had mixed feelings about the concert. I was pleased that something had been staged in memory of Freddie, but still unsure of the event itself. Although I knew Freddie would most definitely have approved, I wasn't sure about some of them performing that day. Quite a few acts Freddie didn't know; I thought the performers were only meant to be his intimate friends in the business. And where was Montserrat Caballé? Where was Cliff Richard? Where was Peter Straker? Or the musicians he loved. Where was Aretha Franklin? Where was Dionne Warwick? Where was Natalie Cole? I don't think they'd even been asked.

That summer, I received the rest of my inheritance from Freddie. Joe, Phoebe and I hadn't been informed when probate was granted; we'd read it for ourselves in the press.

With some of the money I bought a modest, three-bedroomed end-of-terrace house in Stamford Brook and set about redecorating it from top to bottom. At last I had a permanent home again in London where I could keep my Freddie treasures and trophies. I threw myself into transforming the garden and even built a small pool for ten young koi.

I will never forget any of the Garden Lodge cats, but as they couldn't live with me I found myself two new feline friends to take their place – British Blues called Zig and Zag.

My family came over to visit and so did my friends; they were always exciting and warm-hearted occasions. I went off to Italy in the summer of 1992 with a friend; it was a country I'd never been to with Freddie. There were no more chauffeured limousines and being waited on hand and foot, of course. One of the simple joys of travelling, I found, was actually having to lug my suitcase everywhere we went.

Back in London, while I was painting the outside of the conservatory windows I had Freddie's *Barcelona* album on loud all day long. My neighbour asked me to turn the music down, then another neighbour came along and asked if I'd been having a party. I explained I hadn't been.

'What was the music you've been playing?' she asked. 'I sat in my garden listening and really loved it.'

Then a man who worked in a little factory at the end of the garden saw me one day and was even more specific. 'I heard you playing Freddie Mercury's music,' he said, admitting he, too, was a fan.

Since Freddie's death, I feel proud whenever anyone tells me how much they enjoy his music. And I always think to myself: 'That's my man.'

I was invited to the annual Queen convention for the ever-loyal family of fans in spring 1992. It was my first visit to this event and it felt good to be with people who, like me, just wanted to remember and celebrate Freddie as the greatest singer ever, then whoop it up. The fans held a charity auction of Queen memorabilia and one of the lots was a beautiful lifelike portrait of Freddie in oils, painted by a fan. Joe had commissioned a portrait of Freddie, but he had taken it with him. I fell in love with the picture, and bought it and took it home. I had a place for it in mind.

Joe was now going to and from America most of the time, coming back to Britain for his Aids treatment. He'd always said he'd visit me in my new home, but on his flying visits back to Britain he couldn't find the time.

On 5 September 1992, Freddie's birthday, I packed the portrait I'd bought of him at the fan club convention into the car, picked up two dozen red roses for my darling, and drove over to Garden Lodge. I arrived rather early, unannounced, and rang the doorbell. Mary answered and pressed the button to unlock the gate. As I stepped in she came out of the kitchen and walked towards me. For a moment I actually thought she was going to give me a hug. Sadly, when she got about four feet from me her attitude changed. I told her I'd bought a portrait of Freddie at the convention and wanted to leave it, to be hung anywhere in the house she thought suitable.

'I bought it for here,' I said.

When I left a few minutes later, she said, 'Keep in touch.'

Two months later, on the first anniversary of Freddie's death, 24 November, I returned again to Garden Lodge. I rang the doorbell and Mary let me in. I was armed with a bouquet of colourful mixed flowers, the kind of thing Freddie loved, with lots of every different sort. I went into the kitchen and we talked for a few moments. This time, just as I was about to leave, little Miko appeared. She came into the kitchen and purred at me for a few minutes. I smiled at her, but knew it was time for me to go.

Then I was in Chiswick High Road one day, strolling with friends past a restaurant called Tootsie's, when I spotted someone jumping up and down and waving like crazy. It was Joe; I didn't even know he was back in town. I didn't recognise him at first, he'd lost so much weight. His condition was plainly getting worse. We agreed to meet the next day when, over coffee, we caught up on all our news. He smiled a lot, but I don't think he was having a good day on his medication. It made him irritable and drowsy.

We talked about everything that day and the memories of Freddie flooded out of us. He came to visit me for about four hours to see my home. He told me he was planning to set up a small business, perhaps a bed and breakfast place somewhere, and enthused about it. He also said he was planning a trip to Japan and asked if I'd like to join him. I said no. I felt it was one of those places which held just too many memories of Freddie for me to handle so soon. I ran Joe back to his home and we hugged and said goodbye.

About ten days later Phoebe rang me out of the blue. That morning an old friend of mine had died and I told him I was feeling a little down.

'You'd better brace yourself,' he said softly. 'Joe died this morning.' I was shattered; totally devastated. I just couldn't believe it. The shock of Freddie's death hadn't prepared me in any way for the pain of Joe's.

Since November 1991 the three of us had become very close. We'd got to know the chapters in our private lives we'd never discovered when Freddie was alive. From the moment we shared The Mews we bonded into close friends. Suddenly we were all fully aware of each other, both our good habits and our bad. I'm glad I remain in touch with Phoebe, and I'm reassured to think that he's still there.

I went back to Garden Lodge with my crazy bouquets for Freddie in September and November 1993. On each visit Mary invited me in for a few moments. I would have loved to have been allowed just once to take a look at Freddie's garden to see how it is turning out, but it never seems right to ask.

I've heard nothing from Mary since the second anniversary of Freddie's death. I have spoken to her on the phone, but haven't received a letter from her. I try to let bygones be bygones, and when I went to Italy I sent her a postcard. She told me how nice it was to hear from me.

But Mary seemed to have some strange ideas about Freddie's last days. She told me Freddie had lost his sight completely long before he died, but I don't think he had. One day Mary and I were in Freddie's bedroom and I switched on the television. Mary told me Freddie couldn't stand the thought of the television being on, though it was news to me. He and I watched television together on many of our evenings when Mary had gone home, and he never once asked me to turn it off. No, if Freddie's sight did fail him, it only happened on that final Sunday, 24 November.

Mary also said a lot to the press after Freddie's death about how much pain he had suffered. I resent her remarks. I never knew him to complain about his deteriorating condition, not once. And I'm surprised that if he did complain about pain he would only confide in Mary. After all, it was Joe and Phoebe who were giving him his medication. I consider Mary's remarks a slight on the doctors who looked after Freddie so well right up until the end.

Some of my things remain at Garden Lodge. I clean

forgot about the trunk of goodies, including the 'Bohemian Rhapsody' lyrics, which Freddie had got out of storage for me a year before he died. The chest is probably still in the workshop where I was storing it. If not, then I hope the lyrics weren't thrown out by mistake. That would be a tragedy.

While I may not have the original lyrics to 'Bohemian Rhapsody' any more, I do have the original lyrics for 'How Can I Go On', written by Freddie in his own hand. I had a little old suitcase which was full of bits and pieces and I guess Freddie slipped them in there for me one day. On the *Barcelona* album 'How Can I Go On' follows 'Guide Me Home', and I'll listen to them together over and over.

The papers constantly repeated an old quote of Freddie's that everyone fell in love with his stardom. I can honestly say I didn't. He could have been a road-sweeper for all I cared. His stardom was just part of his work and I didn't fall in love with it, any more than he fell in love with my work as a barber.

The final resting-place of Freddie's ashes has become something of a riddle, but I'm pretty sure I know where they are. Maybe two or three months before he died Freddie was sitting in the sunshed, Number 27 bus shelter, with Mary and me, just after we'd fed the fish. He turned to us and said: 'I want you both to promise me to have my ashes buried there, underneath the weeping cherry tree, so I can keep my eye on all of you!' So Freddie's final resting-place should be at Garden Lodge at the foot of the weeping cherry with a rare vantage point over the whole place.

The ashes were not collected from the undertakers for the best part of a year. One report said his parents had collected them and they were on their mantelpiece, but I never believed that for a second. I'm sure Freddie is at the foot of the cherry tree, but perhaps the fact has never come out so as to dissuade fans from turning up at Garden Lodge uninvited.

While Phoebe was making all the cremation arrangements at the North London Cemetery he'd also sorted out a memorial for Freddie there. The plot Phoebe selected was absolutely terrific and cost about £25,000. Initially everyone was in favour of it, but when it came to paying for it, £25,000 was deemed too expensive. The reservation was promptly cancelled. Am I angry? Yes. I'm only explaining this now because if the memorial had gone up, as we all hoped, it would have given the fans the chance to pay their respects in the right setting.

Today I get on with life and rarely have black periods any more. To remember Freddie and our life together I listen to Freddie's music. Tops for me are his two solo albums, *Mr Bad Guy* and *Barcelona*. The Queen song of Freddie's which always sends me is the little love song 'These Are the Days of Our Lives' from the *Innuendo* album. As it's also on the flip side of the rush-rereleased 'Bohemian Rhapsody' single, it could be said to be Queen's final song.

The last few lines of 'These Are the Days of Our Lives' strike a meaningful chord to me. 'Those were the days of our lives, the bad things in life were so few. Those days are all gone now but one thing's still true, when I look and I find I still love you.'

Freddie was the greatest love of my life; I know I'll never love that way again. Although he did love to manipulate, he never tried to change me. And I never tried to change him. I would have loved Freddie regardless of who he was or what he did, because of his remarkable personality. I once asked him why, out of all the people in the world he could have had, he chose me.

He looked at me and his big, brown eyes opened wide. He said: 'You fought me, you won me!'

If I could do it all again there would be changes. Freddie and I never discussed Aids, HIV or anything related to this terrifying illness. If someone's honest with me then I'm honest with them, but the two of us never went into the realms of what might have been happening in our bedrooms before we met. There seemed little point. Today, everyone should know that the disease is sexually transmitted. With

Freddie I never thought we would need to wear condoms. That was a terrible mistake.

Looking back on it, I suppose I should have realised that Freddie was much more likely to be carrying HIV than me. Although he'd had many different partners, it never affected our relationship. I never thought about it. I met Freddie and we were lovers for the last seven years of his life. As far as I'm concerned, our life together started from scratch. People may say, 'You fool!' and I can't stop them. I'd have liked to do it all over again – but this time with condoms.

I'd give anything to spend my time over again with Freddie. If that could happen I would take a much more active role in directing the way his life – and illness – would go. When I opted to stay away from administering Freddie's medication I thought it was for the best, and perhaps in many ways it was. But if Freddie and I lived our time again, I would get much more involved and want to know everything.

Finally, I wouldn't let other people walk all over me the way they did. All the time Freddie and I had our loving friendship I lived with certain people who dismissed me as 'just the gardener'. The same people always introduced me to Freddie's friends as his gardener. Freddie would never do such a cruel thing to me. I feel a lot of sympathy for the modesty of John Deacon, who would declare: 'I'm only the bass player.'

Joe came to me in The Mews one day and said: 'Jim, I want to apologise.'

'For what?' I said.

'For always looking on you as just the gardener,' he said. 'We never thought of you as Freddie's boyfriend.' It went some way to making up for all those cruel years.

I'm not very religious, but I reckon I'll be reunited with Freddie one day, though I've no idea how. When chatting with Joe once, we touched briefly on death.

'Don't worry,' he said. 'If I die before you I'll tell him everything that's been happening down here.'

'You won't have to,' I told him with a smile. 'He knows.'